Japan's International Relations

Japan's International Relations

Takashi Inoguchi

Pinter Publishers
London

Westview Press
Boulder, Oxford & San Francisco

First published in Great Britain in 1991 by
Pinter Publishers Limited
25 Floral Street, London WC2E 9DS

British Library Cataloguing in Publication Data
A CIP catalogue record for this book is available from the
British Library

ISBN 0 86187 076 X
ISBN 0 86187 095 6 (pbk)

Published in 1991 in the United States of America by
Westview Press, Inc., 5550 Central Avenue
Boulder, Colorado 80301

Library of Congress Cataloging-in-Publication Data
CIP data available upon request

ISBN 0-8133-1424-0

Typeset by BookEns Ltd., Baldock, Herts.
Printed and bound in Great Britain by Biddles Ltd of Guildford
and King's Lynn

Contents

Preface and acknowledgments

In this book I have attempted to analyze how Japan conceives and conducts its international relations at a time of great upheaval in the late twentieth century. In tandem with the growth in its economic power, Japan has increasingly been confronted by myriad challenges both from within and without. It is my observation that on the whole Japan has demonstrated a deftness in adapting to international changes, whether of an economic nature or security-related. One might be tempted to say, however, that, if Japan is termed a success in international adaptation, it is largely because its energy has been focused on technological, manufacturing, commercial, and financial activities without duly shouldering international responsibilities, including efforts to sustain a free trade regime, to prevent military aggression, and to inculcate a sense of global community at home and abroad.

This book is my attempt at analysis and synthesis, not at accusation or acclaim. Therefore, I have done my best to reveal the framework within which Japan's diplomacy has been handled. It is up to readers to judge whether Japan's international relations have been handled reasonably well or not. Obviously their judgments will differ, depending on their own differing criteria. This is all the more reason why I leave that determination to readers.

In writing the chapters of which this book consists, I was repeatedly struck by the fact that history matters deeply. No one can escape the scars of the past imprinted on his or her mind. Yet given the speed with which Japan has arisen from a remote corner of the world and given the scale of Japanese influence felt by the rest of the world, it is not difficult to surmise that Japan has had to make almost incessant adaptation without bothering to create *de novo* a meticulously measured chart for navigation. Japan has had to rely much more intensely on its historical learning about the sterility of military aggression, the need for self-reliance and diligence, and the virtue of daily, piecemeal, programatic tinkering and adjustment without an overdose of either ideologizing or moralizing with grandiose fanfare. This theme runs throughout my book as I deal with Images and Roles (Part I), Japan–US Relations (Part II), Power and Interdependence (Part III), Pacific Dynamism (Part IV), and Prospects (Part V).

It is not an easy task to write in English in an environment where, otherwise, Japanese is the almost sole language used in my daily life. This makes me all the more appreciative of the encouragement and assistance I have received from many colleagues in an invisible college that is spread throughout the world. The University of Tokyo's Institute of Oriental Culture where I have worked since 1977 has been most conducive to writing both in Japanese and in English with its unusually liberal and independent-minded environment for those devoted to the academic profession. Hence, I extend my deeply felt gratitude.

More globally, I have had the privilege of serving on the editorial boards of a number of journals for some years. This task has helped me to look at and analyze Japan's politics and international relations from many angles. I am deeply thankful to those journals and editors: Robert Keohane, Peter Katzenstein, Stephen Krasner, and John Odell from *International Organization*: Kenneth Pyle, Kozo Yamamura, and Susan Hanley from *Journal of Japanese Studies*; Bruce Russett from *Journal of Conflict Resolution*; Richard Ashley and Brian Job from *International Studies Quarterly*; Masahiko Aoki, Masahiro Fujiwara, and Kotaro Suzumura from *Journal of the Japanese and International Economies*; Henry Bienen, Kent Calder, and Robert Gilpin from *World Politics*; and Barry Buzan and Richard Little from *Review of International Studies*. Besides the intellectual stimuli derived from these somewhat formal duties, I have had extensive communication with many colleagues. The 'Dialectics of World Order' project involving Hayward Alker, Tahir Amin, Thomas Biersteker, Ijaz Gilani, and myself has given me occasional chances to reexamine many old ideas. The twenty authors of 'The Contemporary Political Science Library' published by the University of Tokyo Press, of which I am the editor, have also given me very useful opportunities to check my formative ideas against others' normally more solid ideas.

In addition to my first teaching appointment at Sophia University's Institute of International Relations (Tokyo), my visiting research and teaching assignments at the Graduate Institute of International Studies (Geneva), Harvard University's Center for International Affairs, Australian National University's Australia-Japan Research Centre, University of Delhi's Department of Chinese and Japanese Studies, Aarhus University's Institute of Political Science, Johns Hopkins University's School of Advanced International Studies, and Gadjah Mada University's Center for Japanese Studies (Jogjakarta) have contributed to my understanding of nations, societies, and international structures. Less formally, my participation in numerous conferences at home and abroad have helped me to make sense of events from different perspectives. My usual enthusiasm for local language learning for as long as my stay allows, whether Korean, English, Chinese, French, Indonesian, or Danish, may have helped me to get closer to the thinking of other peoples in the rest of the world.

More directly related to the individual chapters, it is Yasusuke Murakami, then at the University of Tokyo and now at the International University of Japan in Niigata, who first led me to write more in English by asking me to work together with the Japan Political Economy Research Committee (JPERC). Both he and Hugh Patrick of Columbia University, the two founding fathers of JPERC, showed their exemplary commitment and compassion in moving JPERC toward publication. JPERC produced three conference volumes of essays from Stanford University Press dealing with the economy, politics, international affairs, society, and culture. I had the privileged assignment of editing, along with Daniel Okimoto of Stanford University, the second volume, entitled *The Political Economy of Japan, Volume 2: The Changing International Context* (1988). Chapter 1, 'Japan's images and options', was first presented at one of the meetings of the JPERC series and was first published in 1986 in Japanese in *Chuo koron*, thanks to Tomohiro Kondo, then its editor, and subsequently published in English in 1987 in *Journal of*

Japanese Studies, thanks to Kozo Yamamura, Kenneth Pyle, then its editor, and Susan Hanley, then its managing editor and now editor, all at the University of Washington.

Chapter 2, 'The ideas and structures of Japan–US relations', was written first in Japanese for a special issue on Japan–US relations of the journal called *Leviathan: The Japanese Journal of Political Science* Vol. 5 (Autumn 1989), pp. 7–33, of which I am an editor. It was subsequently translated into English first by myself and then ably improved by Courtney Purrington of Harvard University. I should thank my editorial peers, Michio Muramatsu of Kyoto University, Hideo Otake of Tohoku University, and Ikuo Kabashima of Tsukuba University, for their receptivity to the idea of publishing a special issue on the subject. Chapter 3, 'Nakasone and his diplomatic legacy', was written in English for *Japan Quarterly* Vol. 34, No. 4 (October–December 1987), pp. 363–70, responding to the kind invitation of Yuji Oishi, then its deputy editor.

Chapter 4, 'Trade, technology, and security', was written in 1986 for the annual meeting of the International Institute for Strategic Studies in Kyoto at the invitation of Robert O'Neill, then its director, now at Oxford University. It was subsequently published in 1987 in *Adelphi Papers*. My chapter was also included in *East Asia, the West and International Security*, edited by Robert O'Neill and published by Macmillan (1987) and also reprinted with permission in 1987 in the Pacific Economic Paper Series of the Australia–Japan Research Centre of the Australian National University, where I spent a full winter in Canberra, thanks to Peter Drysdale, the Centre's director, for the three months immediately preceding the presentation of the chapter. Chapter 5, 'Japan's politics of interdependence,' was written for *Government and Opposition* in 1990 at the invitation of its editor, Ghita Ionescu of the University of Manchester, whom I had the good fortune to meet at a Barcelona conference earlier that year. Rosalind Jones, its editorial manager, was a most helpful expert.

Chapter 6, 'Shaping and sharing Pacific dynamism,' was written in 1988 at the invitation of Peter A. Gourevitch of the University of California, San Diego, for a special volume on the Pacific Rim of *The Annals of the American Academy of Political and Social Sciences*. Brian Woodall, then teaching at the University of

California, Irvine, and now teaching at Harvard University, kindly helped me by reading the galley proofs while I was away from Tokyo. Chapter 7, 'Sino-Japanese relations: problems and prospects,' was written in 1990 for the NEAR (Northeast Asian Region) conference at the Center for Asian Pacific Research, Peking University, in response to the invitation of Yuan Ming of Peking University and Frances Lai of Linnan College, Hong Kong. Makoto Sakurai of the Mitsui Research Institute helped me to get there, and Courtney Purrington again kindly improved the chapter enormously. A slightly different version will appear in the conference volume in 1991 from Peking University Press.

Chapter 8, 'Four Japanese scenarios for the future,' was written in 1988 for presentation at a seminar for a study group on Japan's role in development finance at the Council on Foreign Relations, New York. The first half of the paper was then submitted to, accepted by, and published in 1988–9 in *International Affairs*. It was possible only with the encouragement-cum-endorsement of John Roper, then the journal's editor and now at the Western European Union in Paris. The article was further reprinted in *International Political Economy*, edited by Jeffry Frieden and David Lake (New York: St. Martin's Press, 1990, and *The International Relations of Japan*, edited by Kathleen Newland (London: Macmillan, 1990). The original paper was subsequently edited and published in *Yen for Development*, edited by Shafiqul Islam of the Council on Foreign Relations (Council on Foreign Relations, 1991). Islam and his study group members helped me to articulate my ideas and Brian Woodall was helpful in improving the manuscript.

I am grateful to the following publishers, for permission to reproduce the above material: Society for Japanses Studies for Chapter 1; Bokutakusha for Chapter 2 (Copyright held by Takashi Inoguchi); Asahi Shimbunsha for Chapter 3 (Copyright held by Takashi Inoguchi); International Institute for Strategic Studies for Chapter 4; *Government and Opposition* for Chapter 5 (Copyright held by Takashi Inoguchi); The American Academy of Political and Social Sciences for Chapter 6 (Copyright held by Takashi Inoguchi); Peking University Press for Chapter 7 (Copyright held by Takashi Inoguchi); Royal Institute of International Affairs for Chapter 8.

This Preface and acknowledgments and the Introduction were written in English early in 1991; again, Courtney Purrington was very helpful in improving my writing.

The entire manuscript was further scrutinized by Martha Lane Walsh, a friend and an editorial colleague as the managing editor of *Journal of Japanese Studies*, during her off-work days. I am immensely thankful for her help.

All the editors of Pinter Publishers showed enormous patience, understanding, and grace in handling an author not sufficiently experienced in book-making with publishers in the English-speaking world.

My acknowledgments would never be complete without fully thanking the two doctor ladies who have turned out to be crucial to the publication of the book: Frances Pinter and Kuniko Inoguchi. Frances has been encouraging and kind to me throughout this endeavor, even before I was able to come up with the idea of producing the book for Pinter Publishers. Kuniko, my wife, my friend, and my critic, has always been constructive in helping me during difficult phases of writing and obstructive in keeping me from impossible phases of writing.

Takashi Inoguchi
Tokyo

Introduction

Thrust onto center stage of world affairs, Japan presents two contrasting images. One is an aggressive economic player flexing its manufacturing, financial, and technological muscle quietly, yet often effectively, to attain fairly well-conceived national interests. The other is a timid political player with political machinery unable to articulate coherently its interests and position at home and abroad, let alone to exercise its economic power politically to promote its national interest. This combination of economic giant and political pygmy may be of consolation to those who do not wish to see Japanese clout spread to the political world. But a more common reaction is annoyance and anxiety from those worried that this asymmetry weakens the vital alliance between the United States and Japan and concerned about Japan's potential for becoming a stray sheep of extraordinary economic might.

Examples of the former image abound. The idea of Japan as a nation seeking economic hegemony in the world easily sways the minds of many Americans, for instance, when they learn that the total price of land in the Tokyo metropolitan area is higher than that of the entire United States. This image was reinforced when Sony purchased Columbia Pictures and when Matsushita purchased MCA. Similarly, when Japanese automobile firms were attracted by Prime Minister Margaret Thatcher's policy of providing incentives to draw direct investment from abroad, the mood on the European continent was one of apprehension that Japanese auto plants in the United Kingdom were becoming a Trojan horse which would flood the continent with Japanese cars.

There is also no shortage of examples of the latter image. During the crisis in the Persian Gulf, which began in August 1990, the Japanese government was unable to legislate a United

Nations Peace Cooperation bill, which would have enabled Japanese Self-Defense Forces to be sent to the Middle East in order to show solidarity and support for the US-led multinational forces opposing the Iraqi conquest of Kuwait. Faced with vehement resistance from public opinion and opposition parties as well as a sizable portion of the governing party, and manifesting a visible fissiparity and incompetence in its political decision-making mechanism, the Japanese government gave up its effort to enact the bill, at least temporarily, in Autumn 1990. While the Gulf crisis headed toward the January 15 deadline set by the United Nations, the Japanese government was busy with the new emperor's succession ceremony, government budgeting, and cabinet reshuffling. Although Japan's $4 billion aid package to assist the US-led multinational forces and to alleviate the suffering of refugees and citizens in the Gulf region affected by the crisis was appreciated by its recipients, no Japanese flag waved in the Middle East to further strengthen the appearance of solidarity against Iraq. As a result, the salient reaction in the United States was one of dismay and even anger.

When these two images are juxtaposed in statistical terms, resentment against Japan takes on a heightened tone, as has been the case with congressional criticism of Japan during the Gulf crisis. For example, while 400,000 American soldiers prepared for imminent war in the Saudi desert, no Japanese soldiers participated in the multinational forces. While the US government spent $100–200 million per day in pre-war Gulf operations and prepared to spend $1–2 billion per day once war broke out, the Japanese government only implemented its pledge of aid in a piecemeal fashion. Even worse, some Japanese firms such as Sony and Matsushita were spending more money to buy up America than was forthcoming from the Japanese government during the Gulf crisis.

These examples illustrate how Japan's foreign policy is often paradoxical to the rest of the world. In this book, I will attempt to provide answers to some of these paradoxes. In other words, the aim of this volume is to provide readers with an analysis of the making and implementation of Japanese foreign policy. I will also attempt to provide an analytical framework whereby Japan's international relations can be better understood. Although this volume is a collection of articles written between

1986 and 1991, I have taken care to organize it in a coherent manner. This task was made easier, first of all, by the extraordinary continuity of Japan's foreign policy line – that is, one essentially evolving around the Japan–US alliance – throughout the Cold War and post-Cold War periods. No less important, the task was also made easier by the striking tenacity with which Japan pursues its interests: efforts are concerned in those areas where it enjoys a comparative advantage – economic, financial, and technological – and maintains a low profile in those areas where military clout and political leadership matter.

It is my wish that this volume be used not only for teaching and research purposes, but also by general readers broadly interested in Japan, its foreign policy and domestic underpinnings, and its global impact and consequences. Although chapters of this book were written over a five-year period, which included the end of the Cold War, I have attempted to minimize repetition, to update references, and make corrections where necessary.

Part I: Images and roles will help readers better to understand Japan's foreign policy in terms of the images held and roles, actual or envisioned, for Japan to play in the world. Given the strong continuity in Japan's diplomacy since 1945, it is very important to depict these images and roles as determined by its relative position and power within the international system. That is the task of Chapter 1, 'Japan's images and options'.

Part II: Japan–US relations will give readers a clear sense of the history, structure, and psychology underlying this crucial bilateral relationship. As Japan–US relations constitute the core of Japan's diplomacy, it is natural for any volume on the subject to tackle it head-on. Chapter 2, 'The ideas and structures of Japan–US relations', will do that task conceptually. This chapter will examine three contrasting perspectives – hegemonic, competitive, and communitarian – from which the bilateral relations can be analyzed fruitfully in four key areas: security, economy, values, and domestic institutions and structure. Chapter 3, 'Nakasone and his diplomatic legacy,' will delve into an analysis of how domestic politics affects foreign policy as observed during Nakasone's tenure as prime minister (1982–7), a critical period in which the basis for Japan's post-Cold War diplomacy began to evolve.

Part III: Power and interdependence deals with functional areas. Chapter 4, 'Trade, technology, and security', will analyze the increasingly critical juncture (not only for Japan but for the rest of the world) of the areas of trade, technology, and security. The end of the Cold War may give some readers the false impression that much of this analysis is outdated, but, on the contrary, the dismantling of the Cold War justification for restricting the flow of technology to socialist nations reveals a heretofore largely implicit motivation for restricting the flow of technology considered so intimately tied to competitiveness among capitalist nations. Chapter 5, 'Japan's politics of interdependence', will illustrate how Japan uses its economic power to increase its gains and to improve its relative position in bilateral relationships with other countries, yet only in harmony with the stable functioning of the world economy. With vivid illustrations from recent events, the chapter will reveal the basic Japanese strategy in the economic realm throughout the post-1945 era.

Japan's interactions with its Pacific neighbors are taken up in *Part IV: Pacific dynamism*. Chapter 6, 'Shaping and sharing Pacific dynamism', places in context the issues of economic dynamism, market liberalization, protectionism, and bloc formation with special reference to Japan's interactions with Pacific Asia. The problem analyzed is how to sustain the economic vigor of the region while sharing its fruits with the rest of the world. Japan's regional policy is portrayed as one penetrating the two giant economic markets of North America and Western Europe before protectionist/regionalist walls – of either a benign or a malign nature – are built and consolidated, while at the same time enhancing intraregional economic interactions in Pacific Asia. Chapter 7, 'Sino-Japanese relations: problems and prospects', deal with the debt of history, an issue not entirely resolved in Sino-Japanese relations and likely to constrain Japan's room for maneuvering in the region because it has so far failed to provide a satisfactory account of Japanese misconduct in the 1930s and 1940s to Pacific Asian countries. The analysis will focus on the intricate equation of the debt of history, economic interdependence, and the strategic configuration of power between China and Japan.

Part V: Prospects will attempt to look at the world beyond the twentieth century, using four scenarios. Chapter 8, 'Four Japanese scenarios for the future', will articulate some underlying thoughts of the Japanese in their attempts to envision the future world. Using the three variables of the scientific and technological vigor of nations, the neutralization of nuclear arsenals, and the debt of history, four scenarios evolving from the crucial axis of Japan–US relations will be assessed in terms of feasibility and desirability.

Part I:
Images and roles

Japan's images and options: not a challenger, but a supporter

Foreigners have viewed Japan in a variety of different ways at any given time in the past, and this complex image holds true even today. Japan is unusual in the variety of facets its image has. This chapter will examine some of the contrasting elements of this image, analyze changes Japan has made in security and economic policy in the past decade, and suggest some of Japan's options for the future.

While Japan is currently seen as a free rider or a parasitic dependent in terms of dense, it is also said that tomorrow Japanese militarism may well revive and threaten neighboring countries. Japan has the highest level of dependence in the world on oil shipped through the Persian Gulf and is criticized for making no effort to preserve the security of that region. Conversely, the possibility that Japan, an economic superpower, will become a military superpower before the twenty-first century and reemerge as a challenger to the United States, is a source of anxiety. As Maeda Toshikazu, the Ambassador to South Korea, said, 'Both the defense free-rider view and the militarism revival view are wrong. But whether Japan makes efforts toward a defense buildup or not, it suffers criticism.'[1]

The predominant image of Japan's economy is that it is a free rider; that is, it takes but doesn't give. For example, although Japan's capital market is not easy for foreign banks and securities companies to penetrate, Japanese capital is very active in foreign markets. And although the amount of Japanese official development assistance is large, Japan's proportion of grants-in aid compared to GNP is small. On the other hand, some see Japan as a challenger steadily conquering the world market by making full use of its state-led economic management, whether in technological innovation, industrial policy, or world marketing. Between the extremes of Japan as free rider and challenger is Japan as a supporter, a viewpoint not frequently heard. This view argues that Japan should contribute to the strengthening of the peace now maintained under American leadership through the defense of sea lanes in the western Pacific and support of US deployment of new anti-Soviet nuclear weapons in Western Europe. According to this view, Japan should support the United States, which is now facing economic problems of its own. This means that Japan must continue to make steady progress in the liberalization of both trade·and capital markets, as well as taking an active part in making foreign aid and overseas direct investment, syndicated loans, Eurobond issues, and contributions to international organizations, using its high technology and excess capital. Many of these actions can be seen as supporting actions for allied nations with the goal of preserving and strengthening the international system led by the United States.

Despite the wide disparity of images in Japan, it is not unusual for them to coexist. These three images reflect the enigmatic reality Japan poses to the rest of the world and the vast range of options it can take within the international system. Japan has suddenly emerged as a superpower 40 years after its defeat and there is room for more serious contemplation of its role than has been previously undertaken.

Japan's place and role in the world

When discussing a country's foreign policy, it is common practice to relate its place and role in the world. For example, David Lake has used the concepts of relative size and relative productivity in dealing with America,[2] arguing that these factors in the economy largely shape a country's role in international society. In this chapter, I will consider the four types of roles shown in Figure 1.1: leaders, supporters, spoilers, and free riders. Leaders have the greatest relative size and highest relative

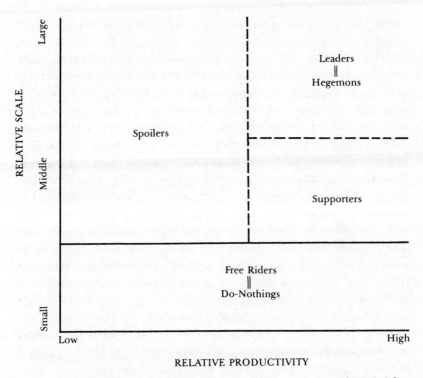

RELATIVE PRODUCTIVITY

Source: Based on David A. Lake's diagram in 'International economic structure and American for-
          eign economic policy, 1887–1934', *World Politics*, Vol. 35, No. 4 (July 1983), p. 522.

Figure 1.1   Place and role

productivity. In order to manage the world economy and the
international environment, leaders devise a variety of arrangements to suit their interests. While leaders bear responsibility
for the principal costs of the system, these arrangements reflect
choices to their benefit. For example, developing countries find
that the IMF and the World Bank are essential international
economic institutions for developing countries facing difficulties
involving the international trade balance and development
planning, but these same institutions also strongly reflect
American power. NATO is a military treaty system joining
North America and Western Europe but, by recently deploying
new anti-Soviet nuclear weapons in Western Europe, it ultimately
serves American interests. International leadership is not a pure
public good; rather, it is a mix of public and private goods. The

international rules and practices possess a certain inertia and continuity preventing leaders from always realizing their own interests because of the need to accommodate their followers.

Supporters are somewhat smaller than leaders in terms of relative size, but they are almost the same as leaders in relative productivity. They support and conform to the international rules and practices built by the leaders, and although they pay certain limited expenses they are usually rather important countries. Supporters are sometimes called 'junior partners'. What must be noted here is that supporters are not blind followers. In cases where the cost of conforming to a leader's expectations is too high, a supporter – possessing the ability to champion its own specific interests – will disregard the interests of the leader. The alliance between a leader and its supporters often has characteristics that can best be described as 'dreaming different dreams in the same bed'. It is not unusual to have discord among the members of an alliance.

The third category is spoilers, whose relative size is much the same as leaders but who are in most cases inferior to leaders and supporters in terms of relative productivity. Spoilers sabotage the international rules and practices and attempt to break them down. Normally, however, spoilers don't attempt total destruction of the system; those categorically opposed to the system are called challengers.

Distinguishing between supporters and spoilers is not always easy. When a supporter becomes non-conforming and asserts its own interests *vis-à-vis* the leader, its actions can easily change into those of a spoiler. Americans thought de Gaulle a spoiler for his withdrawal of France from NATO, and an increasing number of Americans think the same of Japan today because of its economic advances. Michel Jobert, former foreign trade minister of socialist France, categorized the USSR and Japan as spoilers by saying that the world would be much happier without the military menace of the USSR and the economic threat of Japan.[3] On this level, then, the Soviet Union and Japan are in the same category.

Free riders, the fourth category, are small in relative size; their relative productivity can be on a par with leaders and supporters, or it can be low like that of spoilers. For example, almost all of the developing countries receiving the benefits of the preferential tariff rates provided within the structure of GATT may be called free riders.[4]

Which category best describes Japan? In terms of relative size, there are a variety of indicators.[5] For example, in looking at the comparative populations of Japan, the United States, and Europe (EC), we find a ratio of 1:2:2.5. A comparison of GNPs shows a ratio of 1:3:2. A comparison of exports for Japan and the United States shows a ratio of 1:1.6, and for imports 1:2.

Relative productivity is more difficult to measure. Let me present data from a recent MITI White Paper on labor productivity measured in terms of value added.[6] Looking only at the manufacturing sector, the ratio of this productivity between Japan and the United States is 85:100. However, in the three sectors of steel, electronics, and automobiles, Japan's productivity is higher. In recent years, the productivity of a number of sectors in Japan has increased, although in agriculture, the defense industry, and the service sector, Japan's value-added labor productivity still trails that of the United States. Within the industrial sector, however, Japan today has achieved a level of productivity rivaling West Germany, Canada, France, the Netherlands, Norway, and Sweden, bringing Japan close to the role of Lake's supporter category.

Due to the levels of its economic scale and productivity, Japan has come to support and facilitate international economic activity. Here I would like to indicate more concretely how Japan, whose interests are generally met by these activities, contributes to international society. In terms of officially provided development assistance, in 1982 Japan was number four in the world with $3 billion, ranking behind the United States at $8.2 billion, France at $4 billion, and West Germany at $3.2 billion.[7] In addition to aid to neighboring countries in East and Southeast Asia and to those countries that supply natural resources, Japan has also increased aid to countries strategically important to the United States (Pakistan, Egypt, Turkey, Saudi Arabia, and pro-US Central American countries). Whereas US aids supports basic needs (hygiene, agriculture, education) and provides weapons, Japan's aid emphasizes socio-economic infrastructure and basic industries (such as textiles, steel, petrochemicals, and electricity).

In terms of the amount of funds disbursed to international

agencies, Japan ranks number two among members of the World Bank and is on a par with the United States in the Asia Development Bank. Furthermore, Japan supports, in low profile, bank operations aimed at the healthy development of countries that have borrowed money and received aid.

In the category of outstanding net external assets, at the end of 1983 Japan was second at $37.2 billion, behind the United States with $135 billion.[8] Japanese syndicated loans and direct foreign investment have increased dramatically during the 1980s. Japan's syndicated loans, which reached $32.1 billion in 1982,[9] have three characteristics which are appropriate to its role of supporter. First, compared to US and OPEC loans, the interest rates on Japanese loans are lower and the maturity longer. Second, Japanese banks frequently make syndicated loans with US banks and often become lead banks or co-lead banks. In 1983, the Bank of Tokyo ranked number seven in the world as a lead bank; for sovereign debtors (i.e., nations) it held second place; for supranational debtors (i.e., international agencies), it was first. Third, along with the United States, Japan helps with operations to reschedule debts for many developing nations. Japan's direct foreign investment has grown dramatically. In 1982 it reached $29 billion, fourth in the world.[10] Also noteworthy is the overall Japanese willingness to accept minority ownership, thus befitting Japan's role as supporter.

In the trade sphere, Japan is steadily proceeding with liberalization based on the agreement of the Tokyo Round of GATT; for manufactured goods, Japan has a lower average tariff rate than the United States or Western Europe. Similarly, in terms of the number of markets affected by non-tariff barriers, Japan is lowest at 7 per cent, compared to the United States and Italy at 34 per cent, France at 32 per cent, Britain at 22 per cent, West Germany at 20 per cent, and Canada at 10 per cent.[11] Even agricultural products have been liberalized somewhat under external pressure. Japan has been trying to advance free trade with the United States by scheduling a new round of talks while avoiding the withdrawal of Western Europe from those talks. This also corresponds well to Japan's role as supporter. Japan's financial system left behind the systemic inertia of the 1920s' bank crisis and the securities panic of the mid-1960s. But by the mid-1980s, Japan has joined international trends of financial liberalization that date from the mid-1970s. The 1984 agreement reached by the Japan–US Yen–Dollar Committee was a big step in that direction.

With the world's highest savings rate and many internationally competitive manufactured goods, Japan has become a creditor nation. Japanese banks, more directly than in the past, lend large amounts of capital through the Eurodollar market by such means as acquiring a large foreign investment portfolio and greater earnings for Japanese direct foreign investments.

In the sphere of national security, Japanese military spending has increased an average of 7.7 per cent annually over the past five years, reaching in 1982 an annual total of approximately $10 billion (1 per cent of GNP).[12] Obviously, US military spending is higher at $300 billion (10 per cent of GNP), but neither does Japan compare with countries in the 3–7 per cent range such as West Germany, France, and Britain. Japan's total military spending in the past 20 years was $77 billion, similar to that of Italy.[13] In the same period, the responsibilities and roles Japan shares with the United States have grown dramatically. For example, Japan is responsible for American base expenses in Japan, information-gathering in the neighboring maritime area, Japanese–American cooperation in the event of blockade of the straits of Soya, Tsugaru, and Tsushima, and joint military maneuvers in the western Pacific. In politics, in 1983 Japan strongly supported US placement of new nuclear weapons in Western Europe in response to the placement of new Soviet weapons. In 1981, issues between Japan and South Korea were resolved before Prime Minister Nakasone's trip to America, and Japan attempted to mediate in the Iran–Iraq War. At the Western Summit in 1984, Prime Minister Nakasone urged President Reagan to initiate Soviet–American talks. These actions indicate Japan's role as a supporter.

Japan can be seen in each of the roles of free rider, supporter, and challenger. What has brought about these three images, and how do they coexist? There are other factors, but the primary two are Japan's rapid growth and America's reassertion of hegemony.

First, Japan's relatively high growth rate is likely to continue in the foreseeable future. Japanese growth and change have been so rapid that many in the world have difficulty perceiving what is indeed occurring. This is not always the case, but there are many who have outdated perceptions of Japan. Evidence of this is the pattern of 'at first deny, then copy' Japan's achievements.[14] The memories those with such lagging perceptions have of Japan – free rider, dependent, or do-nothing – will die hard. At the same time, Japan's growth has been so rapid that some prematurely and mistakenly believe that in technology, industry, finance, and all other areas, Japan will eventually surpass foreign nations. Because there are people who believe this, a few are beginning to say that sooner or later Japan's true militaristic identity will show itself.

Second, the United States is trying to reassert its world leadership, despite the fact that it is faced with numerous unsolved problems, both domestic and international, and that it is still mired in frustration. To accomplish this, the United States is attempting to strengthen support for its policies from its allies. It is increasing pressure on its allies who are not bearing, in the United States' judgment, a sufficient burden for the alliance. This often takes the form of venting domestic anger against an ally who seems to be managing its affairs rather well. This kind of US policy sees Japan playing the cunning role of free rider, fostering the vague unease among some Americans that, at any moment, Japan will try to become a challenger. At the same time, this has made many Japanese feel that the United States is applying unfair pressure on Japan.

Objectively speaking, these two major factors help make Japan an even better supporter but, at the same time, they cause Japan to be strongly perceived as a free rider and a challenger. Setting aside these three images of Japan, let us here take up the US transition in its international role.

Since the end of the nineteenth century, US economic foreign policy has moved very slowly in the direction of free trade.[15] Between 1873 and 1945, but especially during World War I, the US trade share increased rapidly. Prior to the end of World War I, the United States developed rapidly as Britain's 'junior partner'; US figures for world trade shares were at much the same level as Britain's by the end of World War I. With the development of automation, US productivity increased dramatically in the 1920s. The United States played the role of supporter in the recovery of post-World-War-I Europe. Yet between World War I and the 1930s, America's uncertain role (represented by its non-participation in the League of Nations) indicated that the nation had two roles, supporter and free rider. However, in the inter-war period the United States reversed its junior partner status with Britain. The final stage in that role reversal came when US military forces were dispatched to Europe. American entry into World War II was long delayed but it became possible suddenly because challengers – Germany and Japan – took actions to force US entry. While playing the role of follower to leader Britain and other allied countries, the United States also played a large role in the undermining of Britain's systemic and geographical prerogatives, under the banner of anti-colonialism and free trade. This made the United States and Britain strange bedfellows, or as one scholar put it, they were 'allies of a kind'.[16]

This American role reversal warrants a closer look. It has taken the United States three-quarters of a century to climb from free rider, to supporter, and then to leader. In the process of moving from free rider to supporter, the United States was criticized in the late nineteenth century for sometimes having disregarded the practices and standards of international trade, and it was censured as a free rider for being a predatory late-developing nation. Even in the first part of the twentieth century, the United States was criticized by Britain and other European countries as an undependable, irresponsible free rider. To quote Neville Chamberlain, 'It is best and safest to count on nothing from the Americans but words.'[17] Thus there is more than just a little irony in the 'admonitory' US statements and actions that sometimes paint Japan as a free rider or challenger.

The United States' transition from supporter to leader came about through a mix of mutual cooperation and competition with the leader Britain. What must be pointed out here is that leaders and hegemons usually come from the ranks of supporters rather than challengers.[18] In other words, junior partners emerge as new hegemons from the cooperation/competition with the old hegemons. Looking at leadership transitions since the Portuguese hegemony in the sixteenth century, we see this pattern repeated again and again. It was not the country that challenged Portugal – Spain – which emerged as victor at the end of the seventeenth century, but, rather, it was Holland. The Dutch took up where Portugal left off in that they fought Spain, acquired independence, and inherited Portugal's world trade. In the eighteenth century the country that achieved hegemony was not France (which challenged Holland); rather, it was Britain, which fought France alongside Holland. The country that achieved hegemony in the twentieth century was not Germany, which challenged Britain both in 1914 and 1939, but the United States, which fought alongside Britain. As the example of Britain and the United States before 1945 shows, an old hegemon and a junior partner can become 'allies of a kind'. Whether this same pattern will be repeated in the future is a difficult problem since it largely depends on the international balance of power and particular circumstances. However, because of the very high costs of competition between leader and challenger, it is difficult for a challenger to become a new hegemon.

Above we have looked at Japan's place and role in the world. In the next two sections we will look at Japan's economic and security policies where substantial revision shows that Japan has changed from a free rider to a supporter.

Japan's foreign economic policy

The Japanese economy has undergone rapid change in the past decade, but before examining the nature of this change, I would like to touch on two fundamental developments in the international economic environment. One is financial liberalization, connected with a flexible exchange rate system; the other is protectionism, connected with trade liberalization.

In 1971, the world trade regime supported by the dollar collapsed because the United States, which had created and maintained the system, suddenly abandoned it.[19] It became impossible to maintain a system based on gold to dollar conversion. To maintain the US dollar as essentially the preeminent means of international exchange entailed two major difficulties. One was the high value of the dollar, which had resulted under the fixed exchange rate regime, causing the United States to suffer an increasing trade deficit. The other was that a large capital outflow from the United States occurred, spearheaded by multinational enterprises, causing a reduction in investment at home. This latter development was significant in that it became an important reason for the declining competitiveness of the US domestic manufacturing industries.

The flexible exchange rate system has been in operation since 1973, but as a system it has not been completely trouble free, as indicated by the large shifts in exchange rates that have tended to result in reducing the likelihood of the United States' economic ability to regain its former level of performance. The overvaluation of the US dollar has created serious problems in the past several years in connection with the shifts in the exchange rate. The United States adopted a high interest policy to reduce domestic inflation and to defend the value of the dollar; however, this combination – high interest rates and the high value of the dollar – caused an acceleration in capital inflow to the United States, thus making it a debtor nation by the end of 1984. America's long history as a creditor nation began in 1914 with the outbreak of World War I, when it changed overnight to a creditor nation. Now, 70 years later, it has again become a debtor nation. Once interest rates are lowered to facilitate economic recovery, foreign capital – previously flowing into the United States – may flow out, and the possibility that the dollar could suffer a severe plunge has become very real.

Moreover, Japan is being pressured to open its financial and capital markets. The flexible exchange rate system greatly encouraged the short-term movement of capital and even Japan has not remained impervious to this. Because of the domestic demand saturation in Japan and the large excess amount of capital, Japanese banks, securities houses, and enterprises have begun to aim at foreign opportunities in the form of syndicated loans, issuance of bonds in the Euro-capital market, and direct foreign investment. Overall, the level of Japan's economic dependence on overseas natural resources and international trade and finance increased even more in the 1970s and 1980s.

The second change in the international environment is creeping protectionism coupled with trade liberalization.[20] The beginning of the world recession in 1974 also encouraged the rise of several countries which had not previously been major forces in world trade or production, namely, Japan and the newly industrializing countries (NICs). While the international competitiveness of the manufacturing sectors in the major manufacturing sectors in the major manufacturing countries of Western Europe and North America has suffered a relative decline, the market share of these new countries in the old manufacturing countries has definitely expanded. The industries that have particularly felt the impact of this advance have been textiles, shipbuilding, steel, automobiles, and electronic products. Industrial adjustment has been slow, encountering great resistance, and because of social and political inflexibility these industries cannot be phased out in steps. As a result, creeping protectionism has expanded in the old manufacturing nations. By the late 1970s and early 1980s, one-third of US manufacturing sectors were covered by overt non-tariff barriers. At times, visible protection is imposed, as when Japanese producers of video tape recorders were forced to use costly facilities at Poitier to inspect VTRs imported from Japan to France. At other times, an importing nation can demand a multilateral agreement from an exporter to reduce exports or adopt 'voluntary export control'. Such agreements have been demanded of both the textile industries of NICs and the Japanese automobile industry. Some estimate that if the strongest possible protectionist measures were adopted around the world, then exports from Japan would decline about 10 per cent.

A different perspective toward this problem is how it affects the long-standing members of GATT who maintain the same kind of economic structure and are accustomed to coping with economic problems in the old, familiar way. The threat of protectionism has been used by the older advanced countries to get the newer countries to better 'behave' themselves. Since the 1979 Tokyo Round of GATT, we have seen on one hand a free trade chorus and, on the other, delayed implementation of agreements and creeping protectionism making use of non-tariff barriers.

The two fundamental assumptions of the Japanese economy in the 1960s were turned upside-down in the 1970s. First was the 'small country' assumption, the idea that a small economy exerts little influence on other economies. In fact, the opposite is true. Second is the 'closed economy' assumption. This is the case when an economy is insulated from those of other nations because effective barriers are in place at its boundaries.

The small country assumption has already been discarded. The rapid expansion of the Japanese economy has exerted major influence on the world economy as well as Japan's neighboring countries. Many countries of the western Pacific are strongly affected by the US and Japanese economies. The production and trade of NICs in the Far East have been to a large degree dependent on Japanese investment and capital goods. And for more than half of the countries in the western Pacific, Japan is either the largest trading partner or the largest provider of assistance.

In the world view, more important is the fact that US dependence on trade has increased, and US trade dependence on Japan is significant. Between 1970 and 1980, the ratio of US trade to GNP almost doubled, jumping from 4.4 per cent to 8.4 per cent.[21] It was no longer tenable to retreat into the idea of 'Fortress America' as it was in the early 1970s when the United States departed from the Bretton Woods regime and entertained the idea of energy self-sufficiency. This is to say that because of increased trade and other economic interdependence, it is no longer possible to adopt extreme protectionism. Moreover, since 1977, more than half of America's maritime trade has been across the Pacific, not the Atlantic.

Not only in terms of trade, but in finance too Japan is no longer a small country. From 1981 to 1983 Japanese foreign direct investment tripled.[22] A large portion of this increase was invested in advanced countries, the United States being the largest recipient. Moreover, Japan's syndicated loans and Eurobond issues have been rapidly expanding since the early and mid-1980s respectively.[23]

Thus the closed economy assumption is also unsustainable. In order to understand how Japan headed steadily toward an open economy in the 1970s, it is necessary to look at the basic characteristics of the pre-1973 Japanese economy. An important feature was the compartmentalization of competition.[24] Because of the necessity for a high level of investment capital to meet the needs of enterprises, and because the Japanese economy was essentially closed, financial authorities effectively regulated the flow of capital to targeted enterprises through commercial banks, using administrative and financial guidance. Savings were largely based on quasi-governmental financial institutions such as postal savings. As a result, the financial market was highly regulated while the product market was freely competitive. Thus, competition within sectors was extremely strong while the entire domestic market was compartmentalized. For this reason, the Japanese economy appeared to function with a strange mixture of effective state-led management and fierce competition within the domestic market.

After the first oil crisis, however, the flow of capital was reversed. Instead of capital moving from the public sector to the private, the sale of government bonds moved a large volume of capital from the private to the public sector. The government, because of the extraordinary expenditure pattern born in the rapid growth period, became overburdened and issued large amounts of national bonds, requesting the private sector (securities houses and banks) to absorb them. This reversal in the flow of capital undermined what had formerly been one of the structural supports that gave the public sector the control of the private sector. Because of its high net savings rate of 20 per cent, Japan was able to absorb government bonds without causing the extremely high inflation which took place in America, but high net savings also served to strengthen greatly the private sector's relative independence of the government. Internationally, short-term capital movements became one of the most important characteristics of international transactions in the flexible exchange rate system, and this has become the basis for strengthening the worldwide current of liberalization and inter-nationalization of finance. Nor could Japan swim against the current. This internationalization trend has prompted the crossing of Japan's previous domestic financial methods.

This trend has also resulted, in part, in the rapid expansion of Japan's economy and the high level of its performance. Rapid growth in terms of GNP, gross fixed capital formation, imports and exports, and foreign currency reserves has made it difficult for the Japanese economy to isolate itself from foreign influence. Japan's economic success caused increasing criticism and the demand that its product and capital markets be liberalized so that Japan would protect those markets no more than other countries do. With large trade surpluses and growing market shares in many foreign countries, it was no longer possible for Japan to fight the tide of liberalization.

After the first oil crisis, Japan's good economic performance raised the value of the yen. Indeed, the value doubled between 1971 and 1978. The decline in the value of the yen occurred from late 1979 because of a high US interest policy and increased tension between the United States and the Soviet Union (an actual war, of course, or even the possibility of any kind of war, would reduce the value of the yen) and this trend appeared to continue after 1984 because of Japan's capital liberalization. But there is little doubt that as long as Japanese economic performance remains good, demand for the yen as an international currency will increase. This means that the time has passed when the Japanese economy could be carefully managed and insulated from external disturbances.

When the domestic demand for manufactured goods is saturated, trade friction will rise, and direct foreign investment will increase. When the domestic bond market is finally saturated, then enterprises will draft foreign bonds and Eurobonds. Conversely, foreign enterprises will probably draft yen-denominated bonds in Japan. If net savings stay at their current high rate, then with the increase in Japan's surplus capital will come growth in syndicated loans.

Japan's finance, production, and sales horizons have expanded and enterprises have come to depend more heavily than before on foreign markets. Moreover, these foreign markets do not necessarily witness the fierce competition seen in Japanese markets. Consequently, there will be a long-term decline in improvements in technology, production, and sales unless the following conditions do not come about: first, a rapid and complete liberalization of the domestic financial and capital markets, and secondly, the constant improvement of the industrial structure by technological innovation under which Japan must not become satisfied with producing and selling in foreign markets outdated products that will not sell in the domestic market.

America's experience between the 1950s and 1970s is extremely suggestive on these points. Bewitched by opportunities in foreign countries, American enterprises rapidly became multinational. However, the capital outflow from American banks, which had been lending to multinational companies, became impermissible by the mid-1960s because of trade balance considerations. The Eurodollar market was no longer under US control, developing as an 'offshore' market, and capital outflow steadily continued. The American market was not yet fully liberalized and thus capital outflows continued further when, in 1971, the fixed exchange rate system with dollar/gold convertibility was finally abandoned. The large capital outflow from the 1950s to the 1970s contributed in no small way to America's failing economy and industries.

In short, Japan's characteristics as a small country and a closed economy have been almost completely discarded in the past ten years. It has been a major process: the transition to a flexible exchange rate system (1973), the GATT Tokyo Round Agreement (1979), and the agreement to liberalize Japan's finance and capital markets (1984). And today, Japan's economy is not only extremely large but is also rapidly liberalizing. Second only to the United States, Japan's economic size and productivity will perforce place Japan in the role of supporter. Japan has eschewed the notion that it alone can prosper.

Japan's security policy

Japan's security environment has not changed as dramatically as its economic environment. However, two changes are important: the intensifying tension between the United States and the Soviet Union, and America's growing pressure on its allies.

Relations between the United States and the Soviet Union have shifted from detente to tension.[25] This shift, since the high point of detente in the early to mid-1970s, has been the most important change in Japan's security environment. Since Japan is under America's security umbrella, such changes have an immediate impact on Japan.

At issue is the fundamentally different meaning of detente for the United States and the Soviet Union which makes the two sides perceive the events of the 1970s in very different ways. The United States understood detente to mean the mutual restraint of excessive military buildup, but Americans perceive the reality of detente as unfavorably asymmetric. According to

Secretary of Defense Harold Brown's testimony to Congress: 'We build, they build. We cut, they build.'[26] Detente for the Soviet Union meant American self-restraint in strengthening its nuclear superiority. It is perfectly understandable that the Soviet Union should think that the United States, mired in the post-Vietnam syndrome and in a recession following the first oil crisis, had no choice but to agree to detente and restrain its military buildup. Similarly, the United States viewed detente as the restraint of Soviet expansionism, whereas since the Soviet Union believed the 'correlation of forces' was favorable to the 'progressive forces' of the world, it saw American acquiescence to detente as US self-restraint from actively interfering in Third World revolutions or liberation movements.

Apart from differences in perceptions, growing tensions have also been prodded by domestic developments in both countries. We can point to the appearance of extreme conservative groups of various types in the United States and to the growing non-revolutionary, stagnant conservation of the late Brezhnev and post-Brezhnev years in the Soviet Union.

The 1970s saw the reopening of military tensions and of a large-scale arms race between the two countries. It was also a time of more frequent tensions and conflicts within each camp. In the East, there was the strike and martial law in Poland, the anti-government guerrilla war in Afghanistan, and China's invasion of Vietnam. In the West, problems included the increasing deviation of some Western allies in the direction of what the US government fears might evolve to 'Finlandization'[27] and Japan's economic undermining of the US effort to reassert hegemony and advance its reindustrialization program.

Following the retreat from detente, the United States is now more strongly coordinating policy with its allies. Exaggerating the military threat of the Soviet Union, the United States is also attempting more strongly to align its allies under its schemes in order to restrengthen its own hegemony. The effort the United States is making to reassert its hegemony is focused on three areas, namely, arms, communications, and international finance. The United States of late has especially stressed to its allies its dominance over them in nuclear capability more than it ever has since 1945. America's primary concerns are to see that Europeans are not lured by 'Finlandization' or 'Euro-neutralism' and that Europeans and Japanese, without regard for the second cold war, do not go about 'business as usual' with the Soviet bloc.

As a result, Japanese security policy has been adjusted to fit a different international context. Like the small-country assumption in the economic field, the free-rider assumption of Japan in terms of security has also been rendered obsolete. Despite Japan's rather large economy, however, this assumption of Japan as a free rider was adhered to until the late 1970s. In addition, Japan has been overly conspicuous due to the rapid progress in its high technology industries, from communications to electronics. Japan's economic growth has not been so great, however, as to allow the nation to strike out on its own and 'go it alone.' Almost no one in the Japanese government was impressed by what Mao Tse-tung did in 1957 or what Charles de Gaulle did in 1964. Rather, it seems that most thoughtful members of the Japanese government see Japan's option in the foreseeable future as continuing to be America's junior partner, that is, to be a second-class nation. This is not fundamentally different from the relationship the American government demanded of Japan just before Pearl Harbor. It seems more than chance that the 'Japan bashing' line has overt racist overtones for Americans, evoking the memory of Pearl Harbor. To avoid overreacting on this point, Japanese should understand that demands of various social organizations and interest groups in the United States are articulated directly at the national political level, often armed with a kind of pseudo-logic geared to facile appeals to their clients. As a supporter, then, Japan's course is thus to contribute to US policy as much as possible with its abundant economic resources.

One method by which Japan can perform its role of supporter is to stress the multidimensional quality of national security, adopting former Prime Minister Ohira's idea of 'comprehensive security'.[28] Concealed in this idea is the hope that Japan's contributions to international economic betterment such as foreign aid, debt rescheduling, and contributions to international agencies will be considered supportive of American policy.

Prime Minister Ohira considered cooperative policy with the United States, embodied in the phrase 'a member of the Western bloc', to be a matter of vital importance to Japan. The sudden change in tone in the 1979 Defense White Paper reflected a reaction to American policy changes in the latter part of the Carter Administration. With its policy adjustments, the Suzuki government chalked up a record of 'two steps forward, one step backward'. In a joint Japanese–American communique in 1981, the term 'alliance' (*domei*) was used, and because of the domestic backlash, the government then had to redefine the meaning of alliance to suit its domestic audience. The Nakasone government supported the Reagan Administration's opposition to the Soviet Union. The biggest break with the past has been the strong support for America's placement of new, anti-Soviet nuclear weapons in Western Europe and the linkage of Japan's security with that of Europe and, in turn, global security. Prime Minister Nakasone's support for strengthening Japan's military forces, technological cooperation in military matters, and joint military exercises can thus be seen as a continuation of the Suzuki and Ohira policies. .

Secondly, in Japan's role as supporter, the assumption of an 'Island of Peace' is no longer tenable. This assumption, based on the 'historical lessons' of the 1930s and 1940s, stands as an emotional issue for many Japanese. It says that Japan alone is unarmed, Japan alone has no intention to aggrandize territory militarily, and that foreign countries will thus respect Japan's sovereignty. It may also be called 'pacifism in one country'. Consequently, policy based on this assumption urges restraint from actions that would lead Japan in the direction of a possible military confrontation. Nor has the great appeal of pacifism for Japan's populace since 1945 necessarily receded.

There are three aspects to what may be termed 'pacifism in one country'. First, isolationism assumes that if Japan does not rearm itself or participate in military actions, then peace will prevail; secondly, unilateralism assumes that if Japan single-handedly pursues the course of peace, as stated in Article Nine of the Constitution, then Japan will reap the benefits; and third, free-riderism offers the ironic situation that even though Japan stands under the American security umbrella, it is ambivalent whether to even acknowledge that reality. Japanese worry that the presence of American military bases (either nuclear or non-nuclear) in Japan will invite or induce an attack against Japan by a third country. On this score, the growing number of Soviet military activities since the mid-1970s near Japan and throughout the globe have produced intense discomfort in the Japanese government, which had barely adopted defense plans based on the premise of detente.

In addition, American pressure aimed at increasing Japan's military responsibility has caused the Japanese government to be more aware than ever of Japanese–American security ties. The perception of Japan's fragility and the high costs that would follow a break in Japanese–American security ties provides a powerful incentive for the government to accommodate American pressure and demands. Without this, one cannot understand fully the Japanese government's alignment with the United States in the past several years on such issues as defense co-operation, liberalization of trade, and financial and capital market liberalization. The Japanese government has cautiously acted to accept those demands and, at the same time, paid careful attention to avoid inciting domestic grassroots pacifism. Judging from the government's assessment of the benefits and costs of alignment, the costs of acceptance in economic terms are acceptable, but the psychological costs of getting the Japanese people to 'understand' are still very high. The key words that have characterized the Japanese–American security relationship, such as 'a member of the Western bloc' (Ohira), 'an allied country' (Suzuki), and 'unsinkable aircraft carrier' (Nakasone), indicate the government's efforts to intensify gradually the closeness of that relationship. The policy of security alignment has resulted sometimes in a 'two steps forward, one step backward' quality, while indicating the difficulties the Japanese government faces even now in order to accommodate those who advocate 'one-country pacifism'. Japanese know that the American government all too calmly considers the possibility of jointly fighting wars, while the Japanese government, albeit a bit frightened, has basically supported up to now the course of the American government.

It is difficult to say how far the Japanese government will follow this policy of alignment. When we look carefully at the hopes and expectations of the American government for Japan's self-defense forces (SDF), it is obvious that the current level of Japan's military capacity is extremely limited. But since Soviet nuclear weapons (especially mid-range) have not yet been fixed primarily on Japan in large numbers, the difficult decision as to what kind of long-term defense posture to develop in relation to the Japanese–American alliance is not imminent. In short, the two major assumptions that have controlled Japan's security policy until recently are in the process of being revised in the direction of strengthening Japan's role as a supporter, a response initiated by changes in the international environment and changes in American policy.

Japan's options

The rapid changes Japan has experienced in the past ten years have created a complicated web of images. On one hand, there is an image of a strong economy, adaptable industrial production, and impressive technological innovation. Juxtaposed to this is the contrasting image of political and military passivity. Sometimes the very image of Japan's economic strength and efficiency is uneasily compared to Japan's image as a potential challenger in military and economic matters. In between lies the image of healthy economic growth and political resilience, both contributing to global welfare. Underlying these contrasting images are the increasingly wide number of options envisaged, albeit vaguely, for Japan in the future.

Policy options in the economic sphere can be fundamentally divided into trilateralism and regionalism. These options will be influenced by the degree of protectionism that may develop in Western Europe and North America and the degree of economic development in the western Pacific region. If protectionsim, such as that which has developed in Europe during the past ten years, continues, and if the GATT multinational free trade system breaks down, then Japan will have no choice but to search for and open new markets. Furthermore, should American protectionism develop in the same direction and should America attempt and succeed in bilateral free trade with various countries, such as Canada and Israel, then Japan's policy options will strongly lean toward regionalism. Economic development in the western Pacific region is still insufficient to fill the vacuum that would be created by the 'loss' of North America and Western Europe. Although the growth rate in the western

Pacific region is very high, the level of development of each country is still much lower than Japan's. Even if income levels do rise, the Japanese government will hesitate to independently adopt policies of regionalism given the lack of a geoeconomic land mass core sufficient to support such a scheme. While the western Pacific alignment puts emphasis on Southeast Asia, Northeast Asian regionalism includes Japan, the Korean peninsula, China, the Soviet Union, and Outer Mongolia. The economic dynamism of the Japanese and South Korean economies may well make for a close economic relationship with neighboring socialist countries. Looking at recent trends, we can surmise much of what the future holds in store for Northeast Asian economic relations. But there are many difficulties in increasing dependence on socialist countries for trade, natural resources, and investment, and the Japanese government has largely avoided this alignment.

Despite the two major changes in assumptions, for the foreseeable future there will be no fundamental change in course. That is, basic trilateralism will continue to provide the core of Japanese economic interactions with the rest of the world with the regional components, both Southeast and Northeast Asia, acquiring more weight than they now have but never surpassing that of the trilateral components in the foreseeable future, namely, the remainder of the 1980s. At the same time, Japan's global interest in terms of natural resources and foodstuffs will increase. Fortunately, Japan does not have exclusive economic interests either with Southeast or Northeast Asia. First, only the United States has the influence to force a balance of military, political, and economic power in the region. Second, in looking at an array of aspects such as economic interests, we see that the United States, Japan, and the somewhat reduced EC all coexist in the region, while South Korea, Taiwan, and Australia have recently made economic advances in the same region. Thus, we see little possibility that Japan will assume a position of independent, economic superiority in the region.

Continuation of the Japan–US security relationship and disengagement constitute Japan's basic security policy options. Shaping Japan's policies are the Japanese government's assessment of the Japan–US security relationship and the geopolitical conditions constraining Japan's options. The reasons why the Japan–US security relationship is continuing at present need not be repeated here. Japan's involvement, however, in anti-Soviet actions initiated and led by the United States has become much greater. If Japan clearly becomes a primary target for nuclear or non-nuclear attack by Soviet Far Eastern forces, or if it comes to be widely thought that American troops would not be committed on a large scale in such circumstances, then the Japanese government would have to reconsider the desirability of the security relationship. Looked at in the light of the recent Western European experience when new nuclear weapons were placed there, questions are more than likely to arise on how the Japan–US alliance is to cope with Soviet power.

There are several formulas for possible disengagement from the Japan–US security relationship. There is the example of France, which maintains a close economic and security relationship with America, even while possessing nuclear weapons. This relationship is close, to the extent that it has been said that France is America's best ally. Then there is India, which has taken a position of non-alignment; as a result, in the past ten years world leaders have visited India more often than Japan.

Recently, the idea that Japan should arm itself with nuclear weapons has been broached. This option, however, will entail high costs in order to overcome both foreign and domestic opposition. The most important aspect of this is the American reaction should Japan arm itself with nuclear weapons. Would the United States look on as a spectator if the Japanese government took the policy step of becoming more than a second-class power?

Finally, there is the remotest possibility that, while not possessing nuclear weapons of its own, Japan will carry out a technological miracle and build anti-nuclear weapons which will render nuclear weapons obsolete.

In Figure 1.2, Japan's options are laid out using the two co-ordinates of prosperity and security. Prosperity, or the economic relationship, has trilateralism and regionalism on its axis; security, or the defense relationship, has the Japan–US security relationship and disengagement on its axis. Each quadrant contains a current option or idea: in the upper right is the Yoshida Doctrine; in the lower right is Pan-Pacific Regionalism; in the upper left is

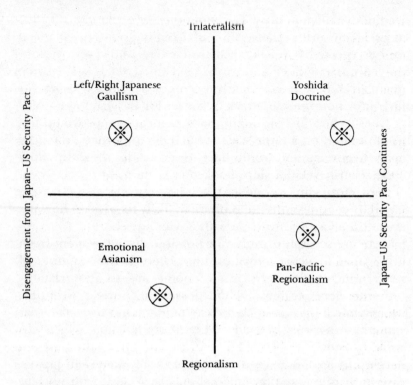

Figure 1.2   Japan's options

extreme left- and right-wing Japanese Gaullism; and in the lower left is an emotional Asianism.

The policies of the Japanese government have shifted in recent years. After the initial heavy reliance on Japan–US security ties immediately after independence in 1952, policy shifted in the 1970s to include an emphasis on trilateralism, on one hand, and the display of Pan-Pacific regionalism on the other. In the 1980s, elements of Japanese Gaullism were quietly added to efforts at strengthening Japanese defense. While it has not necessarily shown up in government policy, the emotional Asianism shared by many people has on certain occasions been manifested in emotional disputes with Americans and Europeans.

Japan is clearly being forced to move away from its former roles of free rider and do-nothing and assume the role of supporter. In other words, the former shibboleths of 'prosperity for one country' and 'pacifism for one country' are under pressure to change. The supporter must be mindful of two considerations in performing its role. On the one hand, supporters are sometimes required to prove their intent by sacrificing for the sake of the 'common cause', but on the other hand, it is necessary to maintain distance from the hegemon's 'arbitrary and dangerous judgments and actions'. A supporter differs from a free rider in having wide options and great power, meaning that the supporter's choice of option affects global welfare as well as its own. Consequently, it becomes necessary to consider more carefully the benefits and costs of those options.

Looking at the major axes of trilateralism/regionalism and Japan–US security/disengagement, it is apparent that Japan must distance itself from the behavior patterns of the free rider in order to perform the role of supporter. Thus, what is needed is for Japan to adopt a positive policy of contribution as a long-term strategy and to carry it out steadily and prudently.

Further liberalization of the Japanese economy is one measure which would alleviate tension with trade partners (more effort should be made to achieve this goal). Other measures which could be considered include: active economic cooperation with developing economies, cooperation with advanced countries in various ways to promote industries, and financial cooperation with both developing and developed nations. Nakajima Masaki's idea of a 'Global Infrastructure Fund' runs along these same lines. To achieve the latter goal is for Japan to act as a large creditor nation and to be such, Japan must be aware of the dangers and risks involved.

The important thing is to articulate the argument that economic, industrial, and financial cooperation would contribute not just to the narrow national interests of Japan, but to global interests as well. Japanese policy has to take on a new spirit; it must extricate itself from the kind of passive, totally self-absorbed policy that mechanically correlates government development assistance or grants-in-aid of GNP, and then expects a direct return on that investment, yen for yen.

One of the goals of a security policy is to encourage a prudent peaceful cooperation that will produce a global nation with the best interests of the entire world in mind, a nation that has not engaged in war for 40 years. Here, peaceful cooperation refers to, in addition to defense assistance connected with the US-

Japan Security Treaty, truce enforcement conducted as part of the actions of the United Nations, supervision of elections, assistance to people in distress, and the shipment of emergency foodstuffs. Foreign Minister Abe's recent proposal for dealing with the Cambodian problem contains the gist of these goals. Peaceful cooperation holds the potential to sweep away the insularity of 'pacifism for one country', allowing Japan to play the role of supporter without necessarily having to run at the United States' pace.

To borrow the words of Amaya Naohiro, pacifism on a national basis is analogous to defending protectionism in the economic sphere.[29] In the economic arena, to argue for free trade, which means prosperity to the world as a whole, and similarly to argue in the field of security for pacifism for one country, which is 'security protectionism', is to invite the charge of engaging in double-talk and supporting neither free trade nor pacifism.

What I propose is the establishment of two new agencies designed to implement these policies. They would be called the Economic Cooperation Agency and the Peace Cooperation Agency. In order to implement the policy outlined above and make it effective, it may be necessary to clarify or recognize the connections between various organizations; for example, in the Economic Cooperation Agency, there would be MITI, the Foreign Ministry, the Economic Planning Agency, the Japan International Cooperation Agency, the Overseas Economic Cooperations Fund, the Japan Export–Import Bank, the Bank of Tokyo, and the Bank of Japan. In the Peace Cooperation Agency, there would be the Foreign Ministry, the Defense Agency, the Ministry of Health and Welfare, the Ministry of Justice, and the Japan Red Cross.

Staff and support for these two new agencies could be flexibly drawn from existing bureaus, agencies, and ministries, as well as from the private sector, in light of necessary requirements specific to each contingency. This kind of institutional reform alone, however, will not have that great an impact. In the context of recent history, decisive change will be realized only by translating Japan's hoped-for role into concrete actions. What Japan needs to do now is not to continue the tired reliance on the power of money and numbers, or a passive foreign policy, but to make a new policy initiative with new ideas and a new spirit that will realize these goals. If my proposal for an Economic Cooperation Agency and a Peace Cooperation Agency results in a set of new policy initiatives, then the purpose of this chapter will have been served.

Conclusion: America and Japan

The hidden agenda in Japan's policy discussion for the past ten years has been 'Is American hegemony over?'. Although American hegemony has somewhat diminished, it will continue in the 1980s. Policies that depend on the Japan–US security arrangement and trilateralism will continue, even while new elements are added to the situational changes. In speaking of the decline of the Roman Empire, Edward Gibbon wryly noted, 'This intolerable situation lasted for about three hundred years.'[30] Pax Americana will probably do likewise. American hegemony will be likely to guarantee international political and economic stability in the short run, but in the long term it does not permit such optimism. How America deals with its mounting economic problems in the next year or two will tell us a great deal about the stability of the post-1990 world.

The relative decline of America's hegemony has expanded Japan's options. The inevitable long-term instability of the international political and economic scene makes it necessary for Japan to develop a long-range strategy. These two reasons make Japan's attempt to select its options increasingly more difficult. How is Japan going to play a role as a supporting actor? What Japan must be is a supporting actor who, without being dominated by the lead actor, can show his own true qualities in such a way as to not only assist the lead actor but to make the whole production a better one. The purpose of this chapter has been to clarify the larger context of Japan's current options and to add concrete proposals so that Japan can perform its role.

Notes

1. *Nihon keizai shimbun*, 20 June, 1984.
2. David A. Lake, 'International economic structure and American foreign economic policy, 1887–1934', *World Politics*, Vol. 35, No. 4 (July 1983), pp. 517–43.
3. Shumpei Kumon, 'Administrative reform requires new national goals', *Economic Eye*, Vol. III, No. 3 (1982), pp. 4–7.
4. *Nihon keizai shimbun*, 26 December, 1982.
5. OECD, *National Accounts*, Vol. I: Main Aggregates (Paris: OECD, 1984). IMF, *International Financial Statistical Yearbook*, 1983 (Washington, DC: IMF, 1983).
6. Tsusansho, *Tsusho hakusho* (Tokyo: Tsusho sangyo chosakai, 1983).
7. Gaimusho, *Sekai no ugoki*, No. 398 (1983).
8. *Nihon keizai shimbun*, 30 May, 1984.
9. *Euromoney*, May 1980, pp. 64–5; April 1983, pp. 24–5; and October 1983, pp. 166–82.
10. *Nihon keizai shimbun*, 14 March, 1984.
11. William Cline, ' "Reciprocity": A New Approach to Trade Policy?' in Cline (ed.), *Trade Policy in the 1980s* (Cambridge, Mass.: MIT Press for the Institute for International Economics, 1984).
12. Gaimusho, *Sekai no ugoki*, No. 398.
13. Ruth L. Sivard, *World Military and Social Expenditures, 1983* (Washington, DC: World Priorities, 1983).
14. Norman MacRae, 'Health care international', *Economist*, 28 April, 1984, pp. 13–17.
15. Lake, 'International economic structures'.
16. Christopher Thorne, *Allies of a Kind: The United States, Britain and the War Against Japan, 1941–1945* (Oxford: Oxford University Press, 1978).
17. Keith Feiling, *The Life of Neville Chamberlain* (London: Macmillan, 1946, quoted by Bradford A. Lee, *Britain and the Sino-Japanese War: A Study in the Dilemmas of British Decline* (Stanford: Stanford University Press, 1973), p. 54.
18. Inoguchi Takashi and Inoguchi Kuniko, 'Dai-ichiji taisen ni itaru Amerika', in Okazaki Hisahiko *et al.* (eds), *'Amerika no seiki' no seisui* (Tokyo: Nihon Keizai Shimbunsha, 1984).
19. Ronald McKinnon, *An International Standard of Monetary Stabilization* (Cambridge, Mass.: MIT Press for the Institute of International Economics, 1984).
20. See Cline, 'Reciprocity'.
21. *Economic Report of the President* (Washington, DC: Government Printing Office, 19 February, 1984), pp. 220, 338.
22. *Nihon keizai shimbun*, 30 May, 1984.
23. *Nihon keizai shimbun*, 7 April, 1984.
24. Yasusuke Murakami, 'Toward a sociopolitical explanation of Japan's economic performance', in Kozo Yamamura, (ed.), *Policy*

and Trade Issues of the Japanese Economy (Seattle: University of Washington Press, 1982).

25. Fred Halliday, *The Making of the Second Cold War* (London: Verso Press, 1983).

26. Quoted in Samuel Huntington, 'Renewed Hostility', in Joseph S. Nye, Jr (ed.), *The Making of America's Soviet Policy* (New Haven: Yale University Press, 1984), pp. 265–88.

27. Inoguchi Takashi, *Kokusai seiji keizai no kozu* (Tokyo: Yuhikaku, 1982), pp. 91–101.

28. Ohira sori no seisaku kenkyukai hokokusho, *Sogo anzen hosho senryaku* (Tokyo: Okurasho, 1980).

29. Amaya Naohiro's speech at the Kyoto Forum, Fifteenth Meeting, 27 May 1984.

30. Quoted in Pierre Hassner, 'Recurrent stresses, resilient structure', in Robert Tucker and Linda Wrigley (eds.), *The Atlantic Alliance and its Critics* (New York: Praeger, 1983), pp. 61–94.

Part II:
Japan-US relations

2

The ideas and structures of Japan–US relations

There is a wide diversity of opinion on the subject of Japan–US relations. Some observers are overtly optimistic about the relationship, whereas others do not conceal their deep-rooted misgivings. Ambassador Mike Mansfield's comment that 'US–Japan relations is the most important bilateral relationship – bar none' is representative of the former view. Characteristic of the latter view is James Fallows' 'Containing Japan'.[1] One reason for these divergent views is that Japan–US relations are so wide-ranging, so deeply intertwined, and so rapidly evolving. Perhaps for this reason, academic research in this field in Japan has not been as advanced as one might expect for a subject of such fundamental importance. Changes in the real world are so swift that academic products tend to lag far behind.[2]

This chapter will show, by way of a critical conceptual analysis, that the subject of Japan–US relations provides the researcher with plentiful empirical data and challenging conceptual tasks. It will attempt to survey critically a whole range of existing research on the subject and provide a new conceptualization of it from four different persepctives: security, the economy, values, and institutions and structures. The analysis presented here will be guided by four policy-related questions. The first two are directly related to Japan–US relations, whereas the latter two are domestic issues indirectly related to bilateral relations:

1. How will the Japan–US alliance evolve in light of the growing US–Soviet detente?

2. How will Japan US economic interdependence be managed in the face of improving prospects for global economic integration?
3. What kinds of values and ideals should Japan and the United States uphold?
4. What kinds of domestic institutions and structures should Japan and the United States create?

Guided by these questions, while describing Japan–US relations in the fields of security, economy, values, and domestic mechanisms, I will attempt to provide a new conceptualization of Japan–US relations in order to point out some general directions for future research that seem to follow from the perspective adopted in this chapter. Each of the four areas will be conceptualized on the basis of the following three levels of analysis: the state, the bilateral relationship, and the global community. These three levels of analysis in turn correspond to three historical periods: the period of American predominance and Japanese subordination, the period of Japanese–American economic competition, and the period of globalization. Rather than answering the four policy-related questions directly, I will attempt to provide a critical conceptual analysis of these issues which are of critical importance to Japan–US relations.[3]

Security

Like many other bilateral relations, the present state of Japan–US relations carries the legacy of war. The Second World War resulted in Japan's convincing defeat and occupation by the US-led Allied Powers for a period of seven years. During that period, the United States attempted to remold Japan on a large scale.[4] The ultimate aims of the United States were, first, to remove the possibility of Japan's reemergence as an initiator of war and, secondly, to place Japan within the US-led, anti-Soviet military alliance network. During the post-war period, US expectations of Japan have evolved through three distinct periods: the occupation period immediately following the Second World War, the Cold War period, and the period of global detente since the mid-1980s.

In the first period, the United States sought to destroy the politico-economic foundations of Japanese military power. Occupation authorities attempted to create a country that was pacifist, agriculturally based, democratic, and dependent on and subordinate to the United States. An image like that of South Pacific islands held under a UN trusteeship may not be far from US aims for Japan in this period.

During the Cold War, the primary goal of the United States was to enhance the economic foundation of Japan, enabling it to become the cornerstone of an anti-Soviet military network in the Far East. For this purpose, Cold War hawks in the United States sought Japan's emergence as an economically robust and politically friendly country within the US-dominated international order. Yasuhiro Nakasone's assertion later in the 1980s that Japan should become 'an unsinkable aircraft carrier' was clearly shaped by this goal.[5] The basic characteristics of the second period have not yet been fundamentally altered.

With the global detente of the third period, as Japan became an economic and technological superpower, some within the United States began to view Japan as a graver threat than Soviet military power, particularly with the growing US–Soviet detente and Soviet economic problems. The emergence of Japanese power is a real source of worry for North American and West European nations as it may jeopardize and undermine their vested interests in the maintenance of the basic rules and norms of the post-1945 world order.[6]

The basic characteristics of the second period remain in force even today. Its major features are as follows: whereas the United States has continuously placed Japan within its global military strategy and alliance network, Japan has intermittently expressed apprehension about the possibility of becoming involved in international conflicts by allying too closely with the United States. It is not difficult to see Japan's tendency not to fulfill its alliance obligations as arising from constraints of pacifist public opinion and a pacifistic consitution. Although the United States tolerated this tendency during earlier periods when Japan was weaker, with Japan's emergence as a great power the United States has begun to view Japan more critically. The US view of US–Japan relations has shifted from that of patron-client to that of competitive peers.[7]

Alliance as a public good

An alliance can be viewed from the perspective of public goods theory.[8] From this standpoint, alliances are viewed as cost-sharing arrangements for providing security, which is seen as a public good. This view would depict the United States as the major provider of security in international arrangements such as NATO, designed to contain the expansion of communist countries such as the Soviet Union. Whereas the costs associated with the provision of security are shouldered primarily by the United States, its allies share in the consumption of this public good. As the power of its allies grows, however, the United States expects them to shoulder more of the security burden.

Extended nuclear deterrence lies at the core of the security public goods provided by the United States. Under conditions of nuclear deterrence, the United States minimizes the risk of a Soviet first strike by retaining the capacity to strike back and inflict major damage on the Soviet Union, thereby rendering it irrational for the Soviet Union to attempt a first strike against the United States.[9] Extended nuclear deterrence expands the deterrence calculus to US allies, which mostly lack strategic nuclear forces, although it is not as convincing as when applied to an attack on US territory.

There are two different views on the effect of nuclear deterrence strategy in the post-war period on relations between the superpowers. No major war has occurred between the two superpowers since their emergence in 1945. One theory asserts that nuclear deterrence has brought about peace, whereas the other view sees no direct association between nuclear deterrence and peace.[10] Furthermore, views differ on whether post-war alliances with the United States contributed to peace. Some empirical evidence suggests that states with an alliance relationship are more prone to war than states without an alliance commitment.[11]

Opinions also differ regarding the shouldering of costs associated with the provision of security as a public good. One view argues that simply comparing burden-sharing among allies during the current period is insufficient. For example, it emphasizes how the United States has shouldered most of the military costs of the alliance since the alliance's inception. This argument places special emphasis on the crucial role the United State played in extending its nuclear and conventional umbrella, at a time when its allies faced severe economic and other difficulties during the immediate post-war period. Views also differ on the division of benefits accruing from the alliance relationship. Debates on the formation, maintenance, and dissolution of hegemonic order reveal two views on this subject. One view holds that US allies enjoy asymmetrical benefits from the alliance, while another holds that the United States receives benefits commensurate with its costs. Such benefits include the hegemon's influence over rule-making within international regimes.[12]

Alliance as a metaphor for sleeping in the same bed with different dreams

An alliance is often viewed as sleeping in the same bed with different dreams. The fact that allies often have distinct, calculated interests can be understood through General de Gaulle's well-known phrase, 'the state does not have friends. It has only interests.'[13] This conception of an alliance is often attributed to Prime Minister Shigeru Yoshida, the architect of post-war Japan's foreign policy. Yoshida believed that Japan, by largely surrendering the task of national security to the United States, could accelerate its national recovery and economic growth. This is often called the Yoshida doctrine.[14] The essence of this idea is that the only way for a militarily defeated Japan to recover its status as a major power was to accept the roles the United States offered it and integrate itself within the political and economic international order organized by the United States. During this early period the United States expressed few suspicions about Japanese intentions, because relative to the United States, Japan was a weak nation. However, more recently, a number of questions have emerged that raise some doubts about Japanese interests. For example, does the Japan–US alliance serve as a means for the expansion of Japanese influence? Or does the alliance serve the purpose of preventing the United States from adopting antagonistic policies against Japan? Or is the United States taking advantage of its security hegemony and treating Japan as a vassal state?[15]

Three factors can be cited for accelerating the diversity of interests between the two countries. First, there is within Japan an emerging view, albeit on a smaller scale than in West European nations, that with the rapidly growing US–Soviet detente, there is less need to take a hostile stance toward the Soviet Union.[16] Demands for a reexamination of Japan's rigid policy toward the Soviet Union appear to be increasing. One manifestation of this is the opinion that the present defense policy of subordinating Japanese interests to the global strategy of the United States should be rectified, a non-provocative defense posture created, and greater autonomy enhanced.[17] Nevertheless, the view that present Japan–US relations should be fundamentally reexamined belongs to only an extremely small minority.

Secondly, Western Europe and North America have started to expand regional economic arrangements in a direction that may be viewed as the beginning of enhanced regionalism. Such steps have led Japan to seek closer regional ties with its neighbors. Underlying this tendency is the recognition that West European and North American regionalism might leave Japan isolated and disadvantaged. In addition, it is seen as in the interest of Japan to encourage the region's development, assure its stability, and enhance economic links between nations in the region.[18] It must be emphasized, however, that this move does not constitute a repudiation of the trilateral structure of North America, Western Europe, and Japan, but rather is an effort to enhance trilateral linkages and at the same time strengthen Japan's competitiveness *vis-à-vis* the other centers. These actions by Japan have strengthened the position of those in other nations who are advocates of economic diplomacy, known in Japan as 'Japan-bashing'. For example, this form of economic diplomacy has surfaced over such issues as the codevelopment of Japan's next fighter aircraft, the Super 301 Clause of the US Trade and Competitiveness Act, rice price liberalization, liberalization of the telecommunications market, and the large-scale retail stores law.

A third source of potential divergence is the values for which Japan stands. This problem concerns the extent to which Japan is committed to such values as freedom, democracy, equality, human rights, fair competition, openness, and transparency. As Japan's influence has steadily increased among Western capitalist countries, this problem has grown in importance. For example, if Japan's South African policy diverges significantly from that of Western countries and is not perceived as advancing human equality, this strengthens the suspicion that Japan may not be fully committed to the same human values as Western nations.[19] Also, if Japan exports to communist countries some technologies considered to be sensitive and gives the impression that it only loosely applies COCOM regulations, this gives rise to doubts concerning Japan's level of commitment.[20] Japan's 'no comment' response to the Chinese military suppression that took place in Tiananmen Square was probably not enough to convince many Western nations of Japan's sincere appreciation of such universally held human values as freedom.[21] Similarly, the more emphatic Japan is on the uniqueness of Japanese practices, the more bitterly it is accused of neglecting universal rules and procedures.[22]

The problem of values is increasing in importance. This is partially related to the global detente process. In other words, in tandem with the evolution of detente, the relative weight of the Western alliance's commitment to international security has decreased *vis-à-vis* its commitment to human values like freedom and democracy.[23] In addition, in an era of heightened awareness of economic competitiveness among Western nations, Japan's commitment to such values is being questioned as part of the criticism of Japan's hard-won economic competitiveness. Unless Japan passes this test sufficiently convincingly, the divergence between Japan and Western nations will only grow.

Alliance as a human community

The perspective that sees an alliance as a commitment to a certain set of values is related to another perspective that views an alliance as a commitment to human community. In conjunction with the development of East–West detente, those values that the Western alliance has long championed, such as freedom and democracy, have become more widespread throughout the world. Although the meaning attached to freedom and democracy varies widely and perhaps more emphasis should be placed on such values as equality and dignity, the point is that the Western alliance nevertheless can be viewed as part of a global human community endeavor toward achieving such universal values. The steadily advancing network of interdependence in both the security and economic arenas bodes well for such a conceptualization. Indeed, the concepts of 'cooperative security' and 'joint custodianship' have become guiding principles of US–Soviet disarmament and arms control efforts.[24] The concept of a 'common European house' espoused by President Mikhail Gorbachev is based on the notion that the security of one country can only be achieved through cooperation with other countries in Europe. This concept enjoys a number of adherents in not only the Soviet Union, but throughout Europe.[25] These are but two examples of how consciousness of the human community has become more strongly expressed in some parts of the world.

The economy

Japan–US economic relations are based on the fact that the Japanese economy has developed from a peripheral economy to a core economy within the 'greenhouse' of the US-led international economic order. This legacy casts a long shadow over current Japan–US economic relations.

Post-war Japan–US economic relations can be divided into three periods. During the first, the Japanese economy developed within the protective US greenhouse. During the second period, Japan was forced to proceed with the gradual and selective liberalization of its market. This liberalization was also carried out in order to enhance its competitiveness. The third period is characterized by Japan's growing concern with the maintenance of global order and the survival of the human community.[26] The first period lasted until the first oil crisis, while the second period lasted until the late 1980s. Although the inception of the third can now be discerned, the present period still contains features from the first and second periods.

What tasks confront Japanese foreign economic policy at this juncture of history? It is evident that the emergence and consolidation of protectionism and regionalism will make it more difficult for Japan to survive unless it accelerates its market liberalization. Since the early 1980s, Japan has become a strong supporter of liberalization by using foreign pressure for market liberalization to accelerate its own structural adjustments and enhance its competitiveness in the world economy. At the same time, since its economic expansion has provoked such negative reaction abroad, it has become much more necessary for Japan to recognize the critical importance of efforts to prove that it seeks to advance fair competition and harmonious relations in the world market.

World market as a public good

The concept of a US greenhouse means in economic terms that the public good of a world market and free access to that market are provided by the United States to its allies.[27] Not only did the United States bear the costs of building the greenhouse, its initiative and leadership were necessary to pay the political and financial costs of maintaining the structure through the creation of international economic institutions such as GATT and the IMF. According to this line of thinking, the world market has only functioned well because the United States has provided institutional support. If one looks at the world market as a public good, most nations and most economies (perhaps 150 or more) in the world can be called free riders. Although institutional guarantees cannot explain everything, the public goods argument as applied to the world market unmistakably advances the notion that Japan is a free rider. The argument especially heightens its tone with the analogy that Japan's alleged irresponsible behavior in the world economy today resembles the US irresponsibility during the inter-war years that helped cause world depression.

There are two kinds of arguments concerning burden-sharing arrangements within international institutions.[28] One view is that arrangements made by the United States should be kept basically intact and only small-scale modifications be made to allow allies to shoulder more of the burdens. For example, this seems to be the premise underlying the relationship between financial contributions and voting weights of member countries of the IMF and the ADB. According to this line of argument, only the United States should have the power to determine the basic framework. Only within the framework of US predominance should some marginal changes be made. The other kind of argument is that voting weights should change in proportion to financial contributions. According to this view, a new coalition of countries will be formed as a transformation in wealth and power takes place (or should take place).[29] The argument goes further to say that if such a coalition does not appear, it should be formed. The following two assertions on the provision of public goods determine the nature of the implications of these two arguments. First, that provision of public goods such as the international economic system can be provided only by a hegemon; and second, that the smaller the size of the membership of the group concerned, the easier the provision of public goods. According to the second view, since the number of members willing to pay the costs for the provision of public goods is limited, it is necessary to create a mechanism for sharing the costs without encouraging free riders in order to have a well-functioning, cost-bearing mechanism.

The world market as a free arena for firms

According to this perspective, the world market resembles a borderless frontier where explorers can move freely. This perspective is somewhat similar to the views that the world market is a society where anarchy prevails or that it is an arena for imperialistic rivalries.[30] It differs, however, in that business firms must take into consideration those constraints that are imposed by the sovereign state on business transactions through myriad regulations along national borders. In addition, it is firms and banks, not states, that are primary actors in the world market. Some state-created frameworks, such as tariff and non-tariff barriers in trade and border barriers in investment and finance, can be overcome by the ingenious efforts of firms and banks. For example, Japanese automobile firms attempt to circumvent import restrictions set up by the European Community by meeting local content requirements through production in the United States and then exporting cars from the United States to the European Community. There is also the possibility that Japanese firms, through military technological cooperation with the United States, may find ways to circumvent constitutional and other legal constraints and manufacture and sell weapons through co-production with US firms or with subsidiaries operating in the United States.[31] As the distinction between civilian and military technologies becomes increasingly blurred, the *de facto* export of weapons is already taking place since Japanese-made civilian technologies are spun-on military technologies used in US weapons systems.[32]

This perspective assumes that the economic activities of the firm are more important than the state. Even more important is the question of what impact the webs of interdependence and interpenetration produced by such borderless economic activities may have on alliance relationships.[33] One view is that interdependence fosters peace or at least mitigates the inclination to resolve conflicts of interest through violent means. In other words, the deeper the economic bonds, the stronger become the voices of those producers and consumers who benefit from such bonds, independent of the state's preference. This argument has many adherents in Japan, a country that tends to look at international relations from a predominantly economic perspective. Representative of this stream of thinking is the blue-ribbon study group organized by Prime Minister Masayoshi Ohira (1978–80). The slogan 'from the battlefield to the market-place' made by former Prime Minister Chatchai of Thailand is based on this line of thinking for the whole Indochinese peninsula.[34] The second argument is that interdependence necessitates painful domestic structural adjustments. As a result, those sectors that undergo hard times or are eliminated tend to harbor ill feelings about interdependence. Thus it may be better to allow certain differences rather than standardizing all the rules and practices of society and the economy. In other words, the forcible construction of interdependence and interpenetration tends to encourage politically negative reactions and is thus prone to malign protectionism and regionalism. For example, trade barriers to Japanese exports may have some positive results since they would not aggravate the sentiment of malign protectionsim and regionalism. Thus, according to this argument, it would be better not to create a system of interdependence and interpenetration of such an extreme nature since conflict resolution would be much easier. This argument is also applicable to foreign direct investment.[35]

The world market as a global commons

This perspective is at first glance the same as 'world market as a public good'. However, there are some important differences. First, this view sees the world market not as something provided by someone, but rather as something those living on the globe must take care of. It is all up to those living on the globe to make it better or worse since all share in the system's benefits. According to this view, the world market is shaped primarily by the core economies. Since the core economies cannot prosper without the existence of peripheral economies, however, those living in the core economies must work toward mitigating the pains and difficulties of the peripheral economies and toward accelerating their development.[36] From the global common's perspective, the tasks of international finance, international trade, technology transfer, and environmental protection should therefore be placed on the shoulders of the core economies.

The Brandt Report on the North–South problem is based on this perspective and the Baker, Miyazawa, and Brady plans were also influenced by this viewpoint. More directly, the heightened awareness of the global environment is best understood from this perspective. Even if business firms prosper, their activities could undermine such prosperity with long-term consequences which were very damaging to all. Increasingly, it is recognized that economic activities can be conducted only under a set of certain constraints, such as limiting working hours, improving sanitary conditions, preventing environmental destruction due to development, forbidding the emission of harmful materials, and preventing environmental destruction by war.

To what extent does this kind of thinking permeate both Japan and the United States? It seems that recognition of these constraints rises belatedly with increases in both countries' GNP. In this respect, the global commons perspective is similar to the public goods perspective.

Values

The problems of values has already been partially addressed in the earlier section dealing with the security and economic aspects of Japan–US relations. In this section, I will examine the problem of values independently of those aspects. In a discussion of the close relationship and bonds between the two countries, it is impossible to avoid a discussion of values. The problems of values constitutes one of the major components sustaining or undermining the bilateral relationship.

Moral leadership

The phrase 'moral leadership' reminds one that the United States frequently used the phrase to set a highly moralistic tone for its leadership and to achieve its ideals worldwide.[37] Although the hegemon's primary role is to create order and stability through enhancement of an international security system and to create world development and prosperity through a free trade system, there is more to the hegemon's role; another important and basic role is the diffusion of its ideals. In other words, the hegemon achieves cultural hegemony. Cultural hegemony is attained when the hegemon expects that other countries potentially could share with the hegemon those values and criteria the hegemon takes pride in and the non-hegemons expect that the benefits derived from sharing those values are greater than not doing so. For example, the constitutions of many countries that attained their independence after the Second World War, such as Vietnam, contain a preamble and/or articles that commit them to values and institutions such as freedom, democracy, and representative assembly. In the same manner, the constitutions of Latin American countries that gained their independence during and after the Napoleonic War included ideas such as liberty and equality from the French constitution.[38] Needless to say, cultural hegemony includes more than political ideas. One might assert that the diffusion of economic doctrines such as a free market economy is roughly proportional to the increase in American influence. One might also assert the economics itself, especially its new classical synthesis, is an indicator of American cultural hegemony.[39] Furthermore, the fact that the English language is a universal language and that Americans are fairly widely liked irrespective of the US government's policies can be cited as good indicators of cultural hegemony.[40]

Relativism

By relativism, I mean skepticism toward the assertion of the universality of American values and an emphasis on nativistic and nationalistic values. Since American values connote relativism in themselves, relativism as used here is different from the normal usage of the word.[41] Relativism means the tendency not to take for granted what Americans say and what is in vogue in the United States. For example, the notion of democracy, Japanese style, is one kind of relativization, even if it is often not quite clear what it means. Since American values such as the American notion of democratic government always carry the emphasis of universality, as is natural with the cultural hegemon, the inapplicability of some American political ideals for the political context of other nations often leads observers to emphasize that Japan is somehow different, special, or unique.[42] However, the relativism evident in American values sometimes leads foreigners to water down further the universality of these values. This may be related to the decline in confidence in American values.

Universality

Values are not diffused unless they have universal appeal even when they have been spread largely by the sword. American values did not encounter much difficulty in asserting their universality. They could assert themselves as the legitimate and natural successor of Western civilization since ancient Greece. Furthermore, it was very natural for Americans, with ancestors such as the Pilgrim Fathers, to promulgate such values with a missionary zeal and to justify politics in moralistic terms and phrases. American values such as freedom, democracy, human rights, equal opportunity, and openness have sufficient universality.

There was another reason why the United States emphasized these values to its allies and friends. It recognized the need for such an emphasis largely because of apprehensions concerning its own competitiveness.[43] In other words, the United States asserted that if its market is open, then its partners in trade, investment, and technological R&D also must open their markets. When the United States was full of surplus energy, it was largely satisfied with being the engine of the world market. But once it began to worry about its own competitiveness, it sought concrete compensation for its adherence to its values. Furthermore, it has asserted such values as if they were universal principles. The need to standardize various rules and practices in conjunction with the deepening of interdependence in order to reduce transaction costs enhances the need for such norms, rules, and principles. Therefore, the US demands have more than a self-serving rationale. Nevertheless, such demands for reciprocity seem to be made on the basis of, and take advantage of, US security hegemony and market size.[44]

It is not clear to what extent Japanese values have a universal appeal.[45] But it is sometimes asserted that the Japanese model with some qualifications may be applicable to other nations. For example, it is argued that the Japanese model is applicable to regions such as East and Southeast Asia in such fields as the factory manufacturing system and labor relations; the Japanese developmental strategy is held to be applicable to East and Southeast Asia; the Japanese model of business firms is held to be applicable to America and Europe; and the Japanese political system may be applicable to East Asia. At the moment, however, such assertions tend to be accompanied with qualifications.

Domestic system

Domestic institutions and structures are very salient issues in Japan–US relations and, therefore, any analysis would be incomplete that did not touch on this aspect. The post-war development of Japan–US relations requires an examination from the following three viewpoints.

Hegomonic and semisovereign states

The United States can be regarded as a hegemonic state,[46] while Japan can be seen as a semisovereign state. The contrast between the two countries is immense. US defense expenditures, which have disproportionately carried the global security burden, are approximately ten times those of Japan, which has tended to rely heavily on the United States for its security. Japan's domestic institutions and structure have developed in a distorted manner, since Japan has relegated its military expenditure largely to support US regional security strategy. Domestically, Japan's constitution, the three non-nuclear principles, and the three principles prohibiting arms exports have effectively prevented Japan from exerting an autonomous military capacity.

An example of how Japan can be viewed as a semisoveriegn state is the scenario that, if the Soviet Union made an all-out assault on Hokkaido with conventional forces, Japan's Self-Defense Forces (SDF) would be incapable of repelling such an attack alone.[47] The Ground SDF would have to cope with the invasion without much amphibious support from the Maritime SDF, which mostly defends the sea lanes south of the Japanese archipelago as part of US regional strategy, and without much support from the Air SDF, which is not capable of defending Hokkaido. The US Armed Forces would stick to their forward defense strategy by attacking Soviet submarimes in the Okhotsk Sea and landing forces deep in the Soviet Maritime Province and Siberia. In other words, the SDF is not capable of defending Japan without the aid of the US Armed Forces. This is because the United States destroyed and disbanded the Japanese Imperial Army and Navy and also encouraged the Japanese government to create the SDF in order to play the role of supplementing and supporting US strategy in the Far East. The four tasks of command, control, communications, and intelligence can function only together with the US Armed Forces. In addition, US bases in Japan function as extraterritorial areas. Furthermore, Japan is mostly dependent on the United States for its weapons systems, as most weapons made in Japan are those manufactured under license from US firms. Domestically, the Defense Agency has not been assigned the kind of role deemed legitimate in most other countries. A large number of the Defense Agency's upper echelons are staffed by officials transferred from their respective ministries and agencies such as finance, police, international trade and industry, and foreign affairs.

Needless to say, it would be a misnomer to call Japan a semisovereign state by looking only at its military capacity. Indeed, it is rare today for any state to be capable of claiming full sovereignty in the classical sense of the word. However, Japan's domestic institutions and structures reflect the legacy of war and the occupation, and as a result Japan can only be aptly characterized as a semisovereign state. This characteristic has led the United States to accuse Japan of being a free rider, or to demand that Japan assume more security responsibilities.

Competitive partners

As a semisoveriegn state, Japan has devoted much energy to economic activities and has, as a result, become America's competitor. What bothers Americans is not just that Japan remains largely a free rider; many Americans have come to hold the view that Japan plays by different economic rules than the United States and that the United States might be playing a sucker's game.

It is not entirely clear why Japan–US economic relations are unfair. But it is clear that Japanese domestic institutions and economic structures are often not very open, making it sometimes difficult for foreign firms to penetrate the Japanese market.[48] For example, the legislative process is not so important as prelegislative interactions, which are kept closed to outsiders. The bureaucracy does not make its policy deliberations public.[49] Japan is also often criticized for following a pattern of protecting with tariff and non-tariff barriers for a certain length of time, those infant industrial sectors deemed essential for national interests, exporting the products once they achieve competitiveness, and trying to consolidate the country's invincible position with a series of intense technological developments. The close collaboration between government and the private sector is also criticized for handicapping foreign firms. The United States has demanded that the playing field be level and has introduced unilateral measures to handicap Japanese firms, such as the US

Trade and Competitiveness Acts's Super 301 Clause, which has been applied to satellites, lumber, and supercomputers.[50] In other words, the United States has tried through unilateralism to induce Japan to behave in a manner that appears fair to it and to remold Japanese socio-economic structures into a more open form. Given the alleged strong hand of the state in framing the institutions and practices of Japanese business activities, concepts like the capitalist developmental state and the strong state have been invented.[51] However, there seems to be a greater need for understanding the behavioral principles guiding the bureaucracy, business firms, and politicians and the expectations determining their interactions.[52]

Functional disparity

I have already noted the steady development of interdependence in the security and economic fields between Japan and the United States. The most important underlying causal force in this process is technological progress.[53] Technological progress improves the destructiveness and precision of weapons so significantly that at least the two superpowers must think about national security in global terms. For non-nuclear superpowers, the superpower-dominated framework remains a given condition. Advances in telecommunications technology have enabled the rapid conduct of business transactions. The diffusion of manufacturing technologies has also become very fast. In other words, an era of 'common security' and an 'integrated world economy' may be dawning.

In tandem with these changes at the international level lies one significant change at the domestic level. Within the domestic political system, there is a fundamental contradiction resulting from two different functions carried out by the state. One is the function of satisfying the domestic population in such areas as the economy, security, culture, and politics. In order to carry out its policies, the government taxes people and institutions and spends money in the form of public policy to maintain the stability and prosperity of national life. A second function is attaining peace and prosperity by managing problems in the increasingly integrated international security and economic arenas. Although both have similar goals, their scope and method are different and sometimes contradictory.

Domestic politics tends to reflect more or less the preferences of the domestic population, whereas the management of international security or world economy requires international managers whose expertise includes special training, technical knowledge, and 'enlightened' international interests. Those managers often assert and advance the interests they deem essential even if they do not take into account domestic preferences and the interests and policies advanced by them tend to favour global security and world economic stability. Such policies can create problems and disturbances for the domestic population and since their domestic base is very weak, they tend to be ignored by the inward-looking electorate.

This functional disparity is a problem in Japan–US relations. A protectionist upsurge based on vested interests and the tendency to put domestic issues first are two salient features of both countries. Furthermore, what appears to one side as the adversary's lack of transparency and overreliance on foreign pressure (the American view of Japanese politics), or to the other side as unpredictability, arbitrariness, and a self-congratulatory system (the Japanese view of American politics), seems to disturb and irritate the other nation immensely. For both sides, the fact that the second function is not very well served by domestic institutions creates frustration.

One of the debates on the nature of the Japanese system is whether the government changes its policy only after there is significant foreign pressure.[54] The term 'reactive state' means that without foreign pressure no external initiatives will be taken. According to Kent Calder, the major factors that have created this characteristic are overreliance on the United States and the fragmented character of the state. To this argument, I would like to add Japan's adaptation through market conformity. Even when foreign pressure exists, the government does not immediately take action. The government waits until domestic conditions become ripe. The extreme example is the domestic apple industry. For a long period after 1945, high tariffs were imposed on imports of apples in order to nurture the domestic apple industry. Only then were tariffs removed. However, since the elimination of tariffs, not a single apple has been imported from abroad because chemicals normally attached to imported apples are banned by Ministry of Health and Welfare regulations.

Market-conforming adaptability means three things. First, foreign pressure must be in the same direction as market forces. Without it foreign pressure has difficulty sustaining itself. Secondly, foreign pressure must also basically conform to overall domestic interests. Without domestic friends and allies, foreign pressure is generally ineffective. For example, rice price liberalization is gradually moving toward implementation only because of the steady decline in rice farming and consumer grievances. Thirdly, when competitiveness is not judged to be sufficient due to the developmental stage of the sector concerned, foreign pressure will not bear fruit if the sector is deemed critical to the state. An example of this includes Japan's attempt to develop an indigenous aerospace industry. It is certainly true that overreliance on the United States and the fragmented nature of the state favors such reactive state action. The state is generally inactive unless it faces outside pressure and criticism. Once this happens, the government waits for some time and assesses how domestic public opinion reacts to outside pressure and criticism. However, once the government identifies sufficient domestic support and makes long-term cost–benefit calculations and proceeds to form a consensus, it slowly starts to adapt to the environment and steadily redirects itself.

There are many Americans who believe in the theory that Japan only changes through foreign pressure and who tend to advocate Japan-bashing. However, among those impressed with the inefficacy of foreign pressure was the young Winston Churchill. When he was Chancellor of the Exchequer in 1927, Britain tried to suppress anti-imperialist Chinese assaults on foreigners with gunboat diplomacy. In response, Churchill said, 'Punishing China is like beating jellyfish. Even if we attack outdated Chinese forts and useless Chinese arsenals with guns, our supremacy will never last anyway.'[55] Churchill's words sound ominous for the attempt to restore US competitiveness through unilateralism.

Notes

1. Mike Mansfield, 'The US and Japan: sharing the destinies,' *Foreign Affairs*, Vol. 68, No. 2 (1989), pp. 3–15; James Fallows, 'Containing Japan,' *Atlantic Monthly*, May 1989, pp. 40–54; Ronald A. Morse, 'Japan's drive to pre-eminence', *Foreign Policy*, No. 69 (Winter 1987–8), pp. 3–21; Takashi Inoguchi, 'Four Japanese scenarios for the future', *International Affairs*, Vol. 65, No. 1 (Winter 1988–9), pp. 15–28 (Chapter 8 of this volume); Charles H. Ferguson, 'America's high-tech decline', *Foreign Policy*, No. 74 (Spring 1989), pp. 123–44, Saburo Okita, 'Japan's quiet strength', *Foreign Policy*, No. 75 (Summer 1989), pp. 128–45.

2. Inoguchi Takashi, 'Gendai Nihon ni okeru kokusai kankei kenkyu' (International relations research in contemporary Japan), *Leviathan*, Vol. 2 (April 1988), pp. 152–62; Takashi Inoguchi, 'The study of international relations', in Hugh C. Dyer and Leon Mangasarian (eds), *The Study of International Relations: The State of the Art* (London: Macmillan, 1989), pp. 250–64, Kusano Atsushi, 'Nihon ni okeru Amerika kenkyu' (American studies in Japan), *Leviathan*, Vol. 3 (October 1988), pp. 190–201.

3. Inoguchi, 'Four Japanese scenarios for the future'.

4. On Japanese studies of Japan–US relations, see Sadao Asada (ed.), *Japan and the World, 1853–1952: A Bibliographic Guide to Scholarship in Japanese Foreign Relations* (New York: Columbia University Press, 1989).

5. Takashi Inoguchi, 'The legacy of a weathercock prime minister', *Japan Quarterly*, Vol. 34, No. 4 (Oct.–Dec. 1987), pp. 367–70 (included in this volume as Chapter 3); Kenneth B. Pyle, 'In pursuit of a grand design: Nakasone betwixt the past and the present', *Journal of Japanese Studies*, Vol. 13, No. 2 (Summer 1987), pp. 243–70.

6. *Nihon keizai shimbun*, 7 and 8 June 1989; *Yomiuri shimbun*, 14 July 1989.

7. Takashi Inoguchi and Daniel Okimoto (eds), *The Political Economy of Japan, Volume 2: The Changing International Context* (Stanford University Press, 1988); Ellen Frost, *For Richer, For Poorer* (New York: Council on Foreign Relations, 1987); John Makin and Donald Hellman (eds), *Sharing World Leadership: A New Era for America and Japan* (Washington: American Enterprise Institute, 1989); Akira Iriye and Warren Cohen (eds), *The United States and Japan in the Postwar World* (Lexington: University of Kentucky Press, 1989); Tetsuya Kataoka and Ramon Myers (eds.), *Defending an Economic Superpower: Reassessing the US–Japan Security Alliance* (Boulder: Westview Press, 1989); Harold Brown, *US–Japan Relations: Technology, Economics and Security* (New York: Carnegie Council on Ethics and International Relations, 1987).

8. Mancur Olson and Richard Zeckhauser, 'An economic theory of

alliances', *Review of Economics and Statistics*, Vol. 48 (1966), pp. 266-79; Jacques M. van Ypersele de Strihou, 'Sharing the defense burden among Western allies', Review of Economics and Statistics, Vol. 49 (1967), pp. 527-36; Stephen Krasner, 'Trade conflicts and the common defense: the United States and Japan,' *Political Science Quarterly*, Vol. 101, No. 5 (1986), pp. 787-806.

9. John Steinbruner (ed.), *Restructuring American Foreign Policy* (Washington: Brookings Institution, 1989); Alexander George *et al.* (eds), *US-Soviet Security Cooperation* (Oxford: Oxford University Press, 1988); Bruce Russett, *Prisoners of Insecurity* (San Francisco: Freeman, 1983); George Quester, 'Dilemmas of common defense', *Political Science Quarterly*, Vol. 101, No. 5 (1986), pp. 733-52; P. K. Huth, *Extended Deterrence and the Prevention of War* (New Haven: Yale University Press, 1989).

10. Yamamoto Yoshinobu, *Kokusaiteki sogo izon* (International interdependence) (Tokyo: University of Tokyo Press, 1989).

11. Bruce Bueno de Mesquita, *The War Trap* (New Haven: Yale University Press, 1981).

12. Robert Gilpin, *War and Change in World Politics* (Cambridge: Cambridge University Press, 1981); Bruce Russett, 'The mysterious case of vanishing hegemony', *International Organization*, Vol. 39, No. 2 (Spring 1985), pp. 207-31: Susan Strange, 'The persistent myth of lost hegemony', *International Organization*, Vol. 41, No. 4 (Autumn 1987), pp. 551-74; Inoguchi Kuniko, *Posuto huken shisutemu to Nihon no sentaku* (Tokyo: Chikuma Shobo, 1987); Joseph S. Nye, Jr, *Bound to Lead: The Changing Nature of American Power* (New York: Basic Books, 1990); Stephen Gill, *American Hegemony and the Trilateral Commission* (Cambridge: Cambridge University Press, 1990); Henry Nau, *The Myth of America's Decline* (New York: Oxford University Press, 1990).

13. Inoguchi Takashi, *Kokusai seiji keizai no kozu* (International political economy) (Tokyo: Yuhikaku, 1982), p. 27.

14. Kosaka Masataka, *Saisho Yoshida Shigeru* (Prime Minister Yoshida) (Tokyo: Chuo Koronsha, 1967); Nagai Yonosuke, *Heiwa no daisho* (Price of peace) (Tokyo: Chuo Koronsha, 1967); John Dower, *War without Mercy: Race and Power in the Pacific* (New York: Pantheon, 1986); Christopher Thorne, *The Issue of War: States, Societies, and the Far Eastern Conflict of 1941-1945* (London: Hamish Hamilton, 1985); Seizaburo Shinobu, *Taiheiyo senso to mo hitotsu no Taiheiyo senso* (The Pacific War and Another Pacific War) (Tokyo: Keiso Shobo, 1988).

15. Ronald Morse, *op. cit.*

16. Takashi Inoguchi, 'Pacific Asia in the post-Cold War era', paper presented to the Tokyo Colloquium on the Future of Socialism, organized by the Yomiuri Shimbun, October 11-12, 1990; Paul Kreisberg, 'Containment's last gap', *Foreign Policy*, No. 75 (Summer 1989), pp. 146-63.

17. Barry Buzan, Inoguchi Takashi, and Chuma Kiyofuku, 'Nihon ni motomerareru hichohatsuteki boei' (Non-provocative defense needed for Japan), *Asahi Journal*, 28 July, 1989, pp. 84–8; Barry Buzan, *An Introduction to Strategic Studies* (London: Macmillan, 1987).
18. Masataka Kosaka (ed.), *Japan's Choices* (London: Pinter Publishers, 1989); Takashi Inoguchi, 'Shaping and sharing Pacific dynamism,' *The Annals of the American Academy of Social and Political Science*, Vol. 505 (September 1989), pp. 46–55 (Chapter 6 in this volume).
19. Yoshida Ruiko, *Nan-A-Aparutohaito kyowakoku* (South Africa: the republic of apartheid) (Tokyo: Otsuki Shoten, 1989).
20. See Chapter 4 in this volume, 'Trade, technology, and security'.
21. *Asahi shimbun*, 15 July 1989.
22. Chalmers Johnson *et al.* (eds), *Politics and Productivity: How Japan's Development Strategy Works* (Cambridge, Mass.: Ballinger, 1989).
23. Charles Maier, *The Unmasterable Past: History, Holocaust and German National Identity* (Cambridge, Mass.: Harvard University Press, 1988); see also Chapter 7 in this volume, 'Sino-Japanese relations: problems and prospects'.
24. Inoguchi Takashi, 'Bush seiken no anzen hosho seisaku' (US security policy under President Bush), *Keizai seminar: Amerika keizai hakusho 1989* (Tokyo: Nihon Hyoronsha, 1989), pp. 46–58.
25. See my essays 'Yoroppa shijo togo no kokusai rikigaku' (International dynamics of European market integration), *Ekonomisuto rinji zokan*, 20 March 1989, pp. 96–103; 'Japanese response to Europe 1992: implications for the United States', paper prepared for presentation at the East–West Seminar, Washington, DC, 4–6 October 1989; and 'Japan and EC: wary partners', *European Affairs*, Vol. 1 (February–March 1991), pp. 54–8.
26. 'Greenhouse' is the word Donald Hellmann uses. On Japan–US economic relations, see Funabashi Yoichi, *Tsuka retsuretsu* (Torrents of currency diplomacy) (Tokyo: Asahi Shimbunsha, 1988); Kozo Yamamura and Yasukichi Yasuba (eds), *The Political Economy of Japan, Volume 1: The Domestic Transformation* (Stanford: Stanford University Press, 1987); Takashi Inoguchi and Daniel Okimoto (eds), *The Political Economy of Japan, Volume 2*; Kozo Yamamura (ed.), *Policy and Trade Issues of the Japanese Economy* (Seattle: University of Washington Press, 1982); Kenneth B. Pyle (ed.), *The Trade Crisis: How Will Japan Respond?* (Seattle: Society for Japanese Studies, 1987); Kozo Yamamura (ed.), *Japanese Investment in the United States: Should We Be Concerned?* (Seattle: Society for Japanese Studies, 1989); Kozo Yamamura (ed.), *Japan's Economic Structure: Should It Change?* (Seattle: Society for Japanese Studies, 1990); Ryuzo Sato and Julianne Nelson (eds), *Beyond Free Trade: Japan–US Economic Relations* (Cambridge: Cambridge University Press, 1989); Edward Lincoln, *Japan: Facing Economic Maturity* (Washington: Brookings Institution, 1987); Edward Lincoln, *Japan's Unfair Trade* (Washington: Brookings Institution, 1990).

27. Charles Kindleberger, 'Dominance and leadership in the international economy', *International Studies Quarterly*, Vol. 25, No. 2 (June 1981), pp. 242–59, and 'International public goods without international government', *American Economic Review*, Vol. 76, No. 1 (1986), pp. 1–13.

28. Inoguchi Takashi, '1945 nen taisei o koeta kokusai koken kokka wa sekaiteki han-Nichi rengo o manekiyasui' (An international contribution state beyond the framework of the 1945 system invites a global anti-Japanese coalition), *Economics Today*, Vol. 12 (Winter 1989), pp. 38–49; 'Kochosareta Amerika suitai, Nihon koryu ron' (Exaggerated US decline and Japanese rise), *Economics Today*, Vol. 11 (Autumn 1988), pp. 177–84; and Takashi Inoguchi, 'Japan's global role in a multipolar world', in Shafiqul Islam (ed.), *Yen for Development: Japanese Foreign Aid and Politics of Burden-Sharing* (New York: Council on Foreign Relations, 1991), pp. 11–26.

29. Robert Gilpin, *War and Change in World Politics* (Cambridge: Cambridge University Press, 1981); Robert O. Keohane, *After Hegemony: Cooperation and Discord in the World Political Economy* (Princeton: Princeton University Press, 1984); Kenneth Oye (ed.), *Cooperation under Anarchy* (Princeton: Princeton University Press, 1986); Duncan Snidal, 'The limits of hegemonic stability', *International Organization*, Vol. 39, No. 4 (Autumn 1988), pp. 579–614; Mancur Olson, *The Logic of Collective Action* (Cambridge, Mass: Harvard University Press, 1965); Robert O. Keohane, 'Reciprocity in international relations', *International Organization*, Vol. 40, No. 1 (1986), pp. 1–27; David A. Lake, *Power, Protection, and Free Trade: International Sources of US Commercial Strategy, 1887–1939* (Ithaca: Cornell University Press, 1988).

30. Raymond Vernon, *Sovereignty at Bay: The Multinational Spread of U.S. Enterprise* (New York: Basic Books, 1971); Hedley Bull, *The Anarchical Society* (London: Macmillan, 1977); Fred Halliday, *Cold War, Third World: An Essay on Soviet–American Relations* (London: Hutchison Radius, 1989).

31. See Chapters 4 and 8 of this volume.

32. Richard Samuels, 'Testimony prepared for the United States Senate Committee on Foreign Relations, Hearings on the Proposal FS–X Co-Development Project,' 10 May 1989.

33. Yamamoto, *op. cit.*

34. Robert O. Keohane and Joseph S. Nye, Jr, *Power and Interdependence* (Boston: Little, Brown, 1977); Saburo Okita, 'Japan's quiet strength', *Foreign Policy*, No. 75 (Summer 1989), pp. 128–45.

35. Ronald Dore, 'Kanri boeki no tsuinin hitsuyo' (Organized trade needs to be confirmed), *Yomiuri shimbun*, 15 June 1989.

36. Immanuel Wallerstein, *The Modern World System*, Vols 1, 2 and 3 (New York: Academic Press, 1974, 1980, 1989); Garrett James Hardin, *Exploring New Ethics for Survival: The Voyage of the Spaceship Beagle* (Middlesex: Penguin, 1973).

37. Walter LaFeber, *The American Age: United States Foreign Policy at Home and Abroad* (New York: Norton, 1989).

38. John Boli-Bennett, 'The identity of expanding state authority in national constitutions, 1870-1970', in John W. Meyer and Michael T. Hannan (eds), *National Development and the World System* (Chicago: University of Chicago Press, 1979), pp. 222-37, Albert Bergesen (ed.), *Studies of the Modern World System* (New York: Academic Press, 1980).

39. Karl W. Deutsch *et al.* (eds), *Advances in the Social Sciences, 1900-1980* (Lanham, MD: University Press of America, 1986).

40. Mushakoji Kinhide, 'Amerikanaizeishon to Nihon: Moho no suryoteki bunseki' (The Americanization of Japan: a quantitative analysis of emulation), *Shiso*, No. 483 (September 1964), pp. 92-102; Albert Bergesen, 'The decline of American art', in Terry Boswell and Albert Bergesen (eds), *America's Changing Role in the World System* (New York: Praeger, 1981), pp. 221-33.

41. Allan Bloom, *The Closing of the American Mind* (New York: Simon Schuster, 1987); Aoki Tamotsu, *Bunka no sotaisei* (Cultural relativism) (Tokyo: Chuo Koronsha, 1988).

42. Yoshio Sugimoto and Ross Mouer, *Images of Japanese Society* (London: Routledge Kegan Paul, 1986).

43. Robert Axelrod, *The Evolution of Cooperation* (New York: Basic Books, 1984) and *After Hegemony*.

44. Inoguchi Takashi, *Kokusai seiji keizai no kozu*; David Calleo, *Beyond American Hegemony: The Future of the Western Alliance* (New York: Basic Books, 1987).

45. Masahiko Aoki (ed.), *The Economic Analysis of the Japanese Firm* (New York: North Holland, 1984); Masahiko Aoki, *Information, Incentives and Bargaining in the Japanese Economy* (New York: Cambridge University Press, 1988). Also see Inoguchi Takashi, *Gendai Nihon seiji keizai no kozu* (Contemporary Japanese political economy) (Tokyo: Toyo Keizai Shimposha, 1983); 'Higashi ajia hikaku seiji taisei ron: Nihon seiji ron e no shin shikaku' (East Asian comparative political systems: a new perspective into Japanese politics), *Leviathan*, Vol. 3 (October 1988), pp. 7-32; and 'Nanamekara mita gendai Nihon seiji taisei ron' (The Japanese political system as seen from an oblique angle), *University Press*, No. 187 (May 1988), pp. 7-11.

46. John Makin and Donald Hellmann, *op. cit.*; Peter Katzenstein, *Policy and Politics in West Germany: The Growth of a Semi-Sovereign State* (Philadelphia: Temple University Press, 1987).

47. Barry Buzan, Takashi Inoguchi, and Kiyofuku Chuma, *op. cit.*

48. Karel van Wolferen, *The Engima of Japanese Power* (London: Macmillan, 1989).

49. John Zysman, *Governments, Markets and Growth* (Berkeley: University of California Press, 1983); Chalmers Johnson, *MITI and the Japanese Miracle* (Stanford: Stanford University Press, 1983); Chalmers Johnson *et al.* (eds), *Politics and Productivity* (Cambridge, Mass.:

Ballinger, 1988); J. David Richardson, 'Economic research on trade liberalization with imperfect competition: a survey,' *OECD Economic Studies*, No. 12 (1989); Paul R. Krugman (ed.), *Strategic Trade Policy and the New International Economics* (Cambridge, Mass.: MIT Press, 1986).

50. John A. Conybeare, 'The use of deterrent threats in international trade', and David Yoffie, 'The empirical study of trade deterrence', both in Paul Stern *et al.* (eds), *Persepctives on Deterrence* (New York: Oxford University Press, 1989), pp. 191–210 and 211–21, respectively.

51. Chalmers Johnson, *MITI and the Japanese Miracle*; Stephen Krasner, *Defending the National Interest* (Princeton: Princeton University Press, 1978); G. John Ikenberry *et al.* (eds), *The State and American Foreign Economic Policy* (Ithaca: Cornell University Press, 1988); John B. Shoven (ed.), *Government Policy toward Industry in the United States and Japan* (Cambridge: Cambridge University Press, 1988).

52. Richard Samuels, *The Business of the Japanese State: Energy Markets in Comparative and International Perspectives* (Ithaca: Cornell University Press, 1987); David Friedman, *The Misunderstood Miracle: Industrial Development and Political Change in Japan* (Ithaca: Cornell University Press, 1988).

53. Miyazaki Yoshikazu and Inoguchi Takashi, 'Seiki matsu seiji keizai gaku o yomu' (Reading the political economy of the end of a century), *Economics Today*, Vol. 4 (Winter 1987), pp. 6 22; Inoguchi Takashi, 'Kokusaika jidai no kanryosei' (The bureaucracy at an age of internationalization), *Leviathan*, Vol. 4 (April 1989), pp. 100–14.

54. Kent Calder, 'Japanese foreign economic policy formation: explaining the reactive state', *World Politics*, Vol. XV, No. 4 (July 1988), pp. 517–41; Takashi Inoguchi, 'Japan's politics of interdependence', Chapter 5 of this volume; Takashi Inoguchi, 'The nature and functioning of Japanese politics', *Government and Opposition*, Vol. 26, No. 2 (Spring 1991), pp. 185–98; Kent Calder, *Crisis and Compensation: Public Policy and Political Stability in Japan, 1949–1986* (Princeton: Princeton University Press, 1988); Inoguchi Takashi, *Gendai Nihon seiji keizai no kozu*; Takashi Inoguchi, 'The political economy of conservative resurgence under recession: public policies and political support in Japan, 1977–1983', in T.J. Pempel (ed.), *Uncommon Democracies: The One-Party Dominant Regimes* (Ithaca: Cornell University Press, 1990), pp. 189–24; Inoguchi Takashi and Iwai Tomokazu, *Zoku giin no kenkyu* (A study of legislative tribes) (Tokyo: Nihon Keizai Shimbunsha, 1987); Takashi Inoguchi, 'The vested interest syndicate: enemy of reform', *Japan Echo*, Vol. XIV, No. 4 (Winter 1987), pp. 56–8; Michele Schmiegelow (ed.), *Japan's Response to Crisis and Change in the World Economy* (Armonk, NY: M.E. Sharpe, 1986).

55. W. Roger Louis, *British Strategy in the Far East* (Oxford: Oxford University Press, 1971), p. 133.

3

Nakasone and his diplomatic legacy

Nakasone Yasuhiro is a man with clear goals. By the time he was named prime minister in 1982, he had accumulated 32 notebooks in which he had written the things he would do when he became prime minister. The 35 years since his first election to the House of Representatives in 1947 were, in his own words, 'a preparatory period for becoming prime minister'.

He is also a man of considerable flexibility, which has inspired the nickname Weathercock. Due partly to his somewhat unorthodox ideas about the Pacific war, the Occupation, and the Peace Constitution, he remained outside the mainstream of conservative politics for many years. His faction (like the factions he belonged to in his earlier days) was rather small. Yet his eagerness to become prime minister led him to acquire those skills of maneuvering and manipulation that warrant the nickname.

Nakasone himself does not mind being called a weathercock. On the contrary, he justifies flexibility as an appropriate principle for Japan in the international community of nations. In the May 23, 1983, issue of the weekly *Shikan Yomiuri*, he is quoted as having said:

What is most important in Japan now is the weathercock. A weathercock's legs are fixed, but its body is very flexible. Thus it can tell the direction of the wind. If its legs are not fixed, it cannot be a weathercock. It is important to have fixed legs and, at the same time, good sense and good judgment. The Greater East Asian War was led by runaway horses that did not have such abilities. Japan needs the attributes of a weathercock if it is to survive despite a vulnerable security system and international economic encirclement. Among the personalities in modern Japanese history, Katsu Kaishu and Saigo Nanshu

[Takamori] are the most weathercocklike, in my view. Those who become weathercocks are truly courageous people. They must not use their abilities for selfish purposes.

When Nakasone was named prime minister in November 1982, he faced two difficulties that had caused his predecessor, Suzuki Zenko, to resign: (a) Japan–US relations and (b) the budget deficit. Although these problems brought him the prime ministership, the same two problems have been haunting him throughout his tenure, and it looks as if he himself could not resolve them in the end.

Japan–US relations

Japan–US relations were at their nadir in the late summer–early fall of 1982. For years, the United States had been demanding that its allies share in the burdens of securing for the common defense. When Ohira Masayoshi was prime minister, Japan explicitly defined its position in the world community: It was 'a member of the Western camp'. After Ronald Reagan became president of the United States, the demands for burden sharing were further intensified. It was widely thought that Prime Minister Suzuki mishandled Japan–US relations. When the governments of Japan and the United States issued a joint communiqué after the Suzuki–Reagan talks in 1982, many Japanese saw the use therein of the term 'alliance' to mean greater Japanese commitment to increasing its security efforts for the Western camp. The US government did not hide its displeasure when Suzuki stated to Japanese journalists on his way back home from the talks that 'alliance' does not mean 'military alliance'. In 1982, it should be remembered, the US economy was experiencing very painful deflation while US defense expenditure was rapidly expanding. Thus the US mood was not favorable to Suzuki's apparent lack of sincerity.

To remedy this situation, Liberal Democratic Party (LDP) leaders chose Nakasone to be prime minister, in spite of the fact that his faction was only the fourth largest in the ruling party. Nakasone, a time-tested weathercock, emerged as a reliable pro-US Japanese politician after his talks with Reagan in early 1983, when he made a firm commitment regarding Japan's further defense buildup. Nakasone characterized Japan and the United States as 'a community with a single destiny' and, in so doing, moved a step toward characterizing the degree of strategic inseparability and economic interdependence between the two countries. Furthermore, he characterized Japan as 'an unsinkable aircraft carrier' against attacks from the Soviet Union. Although this statement brought down the level of public support for him perceptibly, he continued to push for Japan to play a more active role in the common defense. Nakasone used the Western summits to the utmost to dramatize this posture. His outspokenness and strong pro-US stance were impressed upon other leaders at the summit each time he participated, namely, in Williamsburg, London, Bonn, Tokyo, and Venice. His commitment was realized most notably in the Japan–US joint military operation plan and in Japan's participation in the US Strategic Defense Initiative program.

On the economic front, Nakasone's policy was in basic harmony with Reagan's. Reagan demanded an open market, while he killed most domestic protectionist legislation and attempted to appease his domestic audience by using his discretionary power to apply concrete protectionist measures. Nakasone likewise pushed liberalization of the market as much as he could, as shown by the Mackawa Report, which recommends promoting imports; the Japan–US yen–dollar agreement; and the Group of Five (France, Great Britain, Japan, the United States, and West Germany) agreement to rectify the dollar's misalignment with other major currencies. But he, like Reagan, had a major domestic priority. Reagan's was building up defense to restore America's clear superiority over the Soviet Union; Nakasone's was reducing the budget deficit without causing inflation.

The budget deficit

Having been director-general of the Administrative Management Agency under Suzuki – a ministerial post – Nakasone was quite at ease with the continuation of the administrative-financial reform that Suzuki had initiated. This reform had two aims. First, it attempted to adapt budgetary allocations to changed policy needs. Second, it attempted to reestablish the support base of the LDP government. Budget deficits started to accumulate shortly after the first oil crisis in 1973, as tax revenues did not grow very much given the stagnant economy and the predominance of direct taxes in the Japanese tax system. The second oil crisis further exacerbated the difficulties involved in reducing the national debt. To reduce the deficit, it was thought, the public sector had to act to reduce its organizational inefficiencies, hence the steady abatement in public-sector employment by, among other things, privatizing large-scale quasi-governmental bodies like Japanese National Railways and Nippon Telegraph and Telephone Public Corp.

Swollen expenditures became another target of fiscal reform. Social welfare, education, and public works expenditures were particular targets. As life expectancy increases and the birthrate falls, Japanese society is rapidly aging, with a dramatic rise in social welfare expenditures and a substantial decrease in tax revenues in prospect. Hence the need to restrain the expansion of these expenditures is evident. At the same time, the government has made efforts to persuade people to strengthen the ties of family and neighborhood and reinvigorate the spirit of self-reliance in order to make up for the reduction in social welfare expenditures. As the Japanese economy has become sizable, it has become very difficult for Japan not to contribute more to the common needs of the world. Thus defense and foreign aid have been preferred for steady expansion. For fiscal 1982–7 the growth rate of national expenditures by major category was as follows: 36 per cent increase for defense, 37.8 per cent increase for foreign aid, 11 per cent increase for social security, 8.5 per cent increase for education and science, 8.6 per cent decrease for public works, and 21 per cent decrease in subsidies for small businesses.

The administrative-financial reform has not been able to reduce the budget deficit by much, as no measure has been taken to substantially increase tax revenues. As a matter of fact, Ohira's 1979 failure to realize a tax reform to bring in greater tax revenues led Suzuki to attempt the administrative-financial reform to reduce the deficit. But administrative-financial reform has its limits, so after the overwhelming victory of the LDP in the double elections of July 6, 1986, Nakasone gambled on realizing a tax reform that year. He lost the gamble. The hastiness with which the Ministry of Finance and the LDP leaders attempted to see a tax bill passed in the National Diet gave rise to a nationwide tax revolt last winter and spring, especially during the period of the unified local elections. Still, it looks as if the Ministry of Finance wants to try again in the near future. Although Nakasone has been able to adapt expenditure patterns to changed policy needs to a significant extent, the tax reform gamble in 1986–7 will be remembered as one of Nakasone's biggest mistakes.

Foreign policy

It is important to recall that Nakasone is a man of both ideas and the ability to improvise. He firmly believes in a set of long-held views, yet, always conscious of opportunities and con-straints, he reorients his approach to suit the needs of the moment. One of the great ironies of Nakasone politics is the fact that he has been a staunch nationalist, whose obvious dislike of Occupation reforms, the Constitution, and the Japan–US Security Treaty was publicly recorded in his earlier political career, and yet he has emerged as the most staunchly pro-US prime minister since 1945. Another irony is seen in the fact that he loves traditional Japanese values, such as frugality, diligence, and harmony, yet he perceives the need to transform the sectors that represent these values most strongly, namely, agricul-ture and small business. I will show how he combines his old ideas smoothly with new policies to execute what he calls 'the task of overhauling the postwar system'.

The overhaul must begin with Japan's foreign policy, which is predicated upon friendship with the United States. As the United States perceives its own steady decline, and as it grows even more annoyed by its allies' insufficient efforts to work together for the common good, it places increasing pressure on them to share its burdens. Two kinds of demand may be dis-cerned during the Reagan presidency. One is concerned with reinforcing economic reciprocity, while the other is concerned with enhancing strategic integration through interoperability of forces and technological cooperation.

With the steady increase of economic interdependence

between the world's two largest economies, the United States has felt it necessary to make Japan more conscious of the reciprocity in terms of opening its economic and financial markets to the outside world. As the United States was implementing the policy of deregulation at home, it soon turned to pressing its foreign partners to do the same, especially Japan. The United States assumed that since it was doing well with many countries in trade and financial matters, but not with Japan, something in Japan's domestic practices and institutions must have been unfair.

The opening of Japan's financial market has gone fairly smoothly. Not so the opening of Japan's economic market. Though the personal friendship between Reagan and Nakasone has often been helpful in diffusing or diverting intense feelings for protectionism, two factors have strengthened the tone of the US demand. First, the US economy has been experiencing two massive deficits – a budget deficit and a trade deficit – that are unprecedented. Those sectors hardest hit by the consequent economic restructuring have spoken harshly against some foreign trade partners, most notably Japan. Secondly, the Republican administration has embarked on a *laissez-faire* policy and the Republican president has often blocked the protectionist legislation advanced by the less competitive sectors and their Democratic sponsors. The extreme frustration of those sectors is easy to understand. What Nakasone has had to deal with are a series of irritating protectionist moves by a Democrat-dominated US Congress and occasional administrative moves toward satisfying protectionist forces.

The United States has been building up defense since the last days of the Carter presidency, and this has been endorsed emphatically by Reagan. The United States has not only made extraordinary efforts to surpass the Soviet Union but has also attempted to reinforce its alliance network with all the influence it can mobilize. It has been strengthening integration with allies' forces through joint military exercises and joint operation plans in the name of interoperability. Furthermore, with the increased ability of the Japanese to produce high-tech products, it has been keen to advance technological cooperation with the Japanese in weapons development under its leadership. Most noteworthy among the fruits of these efforts is Japanese participation in the US Strategic Defense Initiative program. Another, at the core of the joint defense plan for the western Pacific, is the Japanese role of detecting the movement of nuclear-armed Soviet submarines and Soviet ships and fighter planes. The increasing weight of sea and air forces in the Japanese Self-Defense Forces, long dominated by land forces, is directly correlated with the increasing strategic integration with the United States.

The post-war system

Nakasone sees American demands as providing a golden opportunity to overhaul the post-war system. By *post-war system* he means Japan's semisovereign international status. Instead of taking issue with the United States over its treating Japan as a quasi-vassal state, Nakasone has found that extending the fullest possible support to the United States helps establish Japan's equal partnership. To justify opening the Japanese market and increasing Japan–US military cooperation, he has exploited fledgling nationalism. With the steady rise of their country's economic clout, the Japanese have come to search for something to ease their minds, living as they do with 'a vulnerable security system and international economic encirclement'.

The Japanese nation, like a weathercock, must have a fixed part, according to Nakasone. That is nothing other than national identity. If Japan has sturdy nationalist legs, it can respond flexibly when squalls and trade winds blow. Thus, Nakasone preaches that a big country is responsible for promoting what he calls internationalization. The responsibility is not imposed by the United States or any other country but undertaken proudly by a nation that sees 'its glorious place in the global community of nations'. It is not accidental that daily morning dramas aired by NHK, the public broadcasting system, in the last few years have echoed a fledgling grass-roots nationalism, emphasizing such values as commitment to family and neighborhood, diligence, frugality, perseverance, tenacity, deference to the elderly, cooperation, and conciliation and reminding everyone of the hardships of the pre-war, wartime, and immediate post-war years of all of those who are over 40 years old. Two such dramas, *Oshin* and *Hanekomma*, were reportedly watched by 20 million to 50 million people every day. Nakasone has commissioned an educational committee to overhaul the post-war system of egalitarian and internationalist principles in education. Of the many goals of the educational reform, the ones that are most Nakasone-like in character involve the effort to inculcate a clear national identity in the Japanese, who have been exposed increasingly to the pressures from abroad to standardize Japanese institutions and practices and make them more acceptable internationally.

Though the pressures from abroad in both trade and defense have been strong, Nakasone believes they have produced beneficial effects. Pressures for economic liberalization make Japanese industries more competitive and strengthen the horizontal interdependence of the Japanese economy with other economies. Pressures for strategic integration make Japan 'an ordinary country' and thus less vulnerable to accusations from the Western camp, at least in Nakasone's view.

In reality things have not gone as Nakasone has envisaged. Two events have made this plain. First, the Iran–Iraq war has made innocent passage of the Persian Gulf difficult, as the United States has been very hostile to Iran. The fact is that US forces are stationed there to protect the larger interests of the Western camp, and some Americans are vexed because Japan, the major importer of the petroleum that passes through the Persian Gulf, has not placed any armed forces there. Secondly, Toshiba Machine Co. has sold its milling machines to the Soviet Union, which in turn allegedly used them to upgrade its submarines. This case has ignited extreme anger on the part of some Americans, who resent not only the Japanese adoption of trading practices aimed solely, it seems to them, at making a profit but also what they see as the Japanese betrayal of alliance. It is ironic that these two events took place near the end of Nakasone's term as prime minister.

Domestic policy

Nakasone sees foreign pressure as a means to implement his reforms, the need for which is highlighted by the budget deficit.

Besides the administrative-financial reform, which he has been promoting for years, two additional reforms have been attempted: educational reform and tax reform. All bear on the domestic societal restructuring Nakasone has in mind.

Administrative-financial reform has had many effects. The most important is the restructuring of expenditure patterns to inhibit the expansion of social welfare, education, and public works expenditures. No less important is the privatization of public enterprises and the concomitant weakening of trade unions. Economic liberalization has accelerated industrial adjustment in such sectors as shipbuilding, steel, petrochemicals, and automobiles, with an accompanying diversion of resources to high-tech and service sectors with relatively low unionization rates. This has demonstrably reduced the strength of the labor unions throughout the Nakasone term in office, particularly since the unions of public-sector employees have traditionally been the largest and most militant. Thirdly, the decrease in subsidies to agriculture and small businesses is important, since these two sectors are the slowest to adapt to the forces of internationalization. Yet they provide the most loyal support for LDP policies. With steady liberalization both in agriculture and in distribution areas where small businesses tenaciously hold on, Nakasone has been trying to shift the power base of the LDP from these traditional conservative strongholds to the urban middle-of-the-road wage earners.

In educational reform the most important issues are not only the inculcation of national identity, which I have already discussed, but also the creation of new educational and research-and-development systems. Nakasone's goal is to create a 'high technology–high information society', where the Japanese economy produces high-value-added, high-tech products and the Japanese society is a center for global information flow. To create cadres for that society, Nakasone sees the need to restructure and enhance educational and R&D capacities. As the post-war system means egalitarianism in education, educational reform means finding discriminatory mechanisms to create elites without alienating the vast majority of the people.

Nakasone's third reform effort has been directed at the tax system. Tax reform is intended to increase tax revenues, first, to sustain social welfare expenditures, which are most likely to increase drastically in a rapidly aging society, and second, to enable higher priority expenditures in such areas as defense, foreign aid, and science and technology, which must expand in view of the increasing need to enhance Japan's contribution to the rest of the world and to raise Japan's technological competitiveness. Another important goal is to make taxes more equitable for middle- and high-level wage earners, whose votes the LDP increasingly seeks, and to reduce the privileges accorded to farmers, small-business people, and *rentiers*. Unfortunately for Nakasone, the tax revolt that shook the nation last spring even included wage earners, who saw his tax bill as a means to increase their tax burdens, not as a means to decrease them.

Future tasks

In charting the path for Japan's future, Nakasone's initial strategy of opting for financial retrenchment and a strong pro-US policy were judged *circa* 1983 by many Japanese leaders to be basically correct. But looking at it from the vantage point of the summer of 1987 leads me to a somewhat different conclusion. What has happened in the last five years? First, Japanese economic and financial power has expanded enormously. No one can deny that in the 1980s Japan has become a global economic power. Due in part to the effect of tight macroeconomic management, growth based on an export-oriented economy has been accentuated and a large amount of savings have been invested in the United States, largely through purchases of US Treasury bonds, to take advantage of interest and exchange rate differences. Exports have produced a huge Japanese trade surplus, while Japanese portfolio investment has increased the foreign indebtedness of the US government. Both exports and investment have aroused enmity abroad. When the US trade deficit was the major problem in Japan–US relations, US criticism centered on fairness in trading practices. Adding financial indebtedness to the trade deficit has intensified the hostility, and it rises to incredible heights when Japanese trading practices are associated in the minds of many Americans with the betrayal of the United States and the Western camp, as in Toshiba Machine Co.'s sale of security-sensitive products to the Soviet Union.

Secondly, the Japanese Self-Defense Forces have become an indispensable component of the US global military strategy. Due in part to the consciously pursued policy of supporting Reagan's proposals, Japan's security has become much more closely intertwined with that of the United States. Needless to say, Japan's responsibilities are confined to Japan and its adjacent waters in the western Pacific and do not extend beyond. Moreover, the Japanese Self-Defense Forces limit their mission to defensive tasks. The problem is that with the growing strategic integration with the United States, Japan is increasingly thinking of its global role, and with the sophisticated weapons it has accordingly acquired, Japan has found it increasingly difficult to distinguish between defensive and offensive tasks. Although these changes collide with Japanese pacifistic sentiments, the growing Japanese nationalism may reconcile the contradictions in the future. Whether Japanese nationalism can live happily and peacefully with the incontrovertible economic interdependence is yet to be seen. In a similar vein, no one is sure whether the frustrated Americans can live happily and peacefully with that same interdependence themselves, as their country's clout is slowly shrinking.

Nakasone is a good weathercock. He suits the needs of Japan at a time of a transition. He has been successful in creating a 'fixed part' by fostering national pride and responsibility. He has been successful in pointing the nation in an appropriate direction when the United States, the widely acknowledged leader, is declining and Japan itself is on the rise. The two difficulties that brought Nakasone to the prime ministership have not been managed well toward the end of his tenure. They are likely to haunt his successors and force them to deal with even more heightened tensions than the 1987 Japan–US rows have produced. Finally, he has raised a third problem which his successors must wrestle with: the more serious task of making Japan into 'an ordinary country'. Nakasone politics will be remembered for leaving immense tasks ahead.

Part III:
Power and interdependence

4

Trade, technology, and security: implications for East Asia and the West

Introduction

Perhaps at no other time in history have trade, technology and security been intertwined more closely than they are today. A good illustration of this is provided by a recent Japan–US agreement on semi-conductors.[1] For some considerable time Japan and the United States have been competing very hard in this area, and Japan is clearly catching up. Responding to accusations by US semi-conductor producers that Japanese producers were dumping their products on the US market and to the demands for action under Article 301 of the US Trade Act, the United States and Japan have recently agreed that the anti-dumping cases against the Japanese semi-conductor producers of the EPROM and 256K DRAM semi-conductors be suspended, provided that:

1. the Department of Commerce monitor all the quarterly statistics on Japan's production and sales of EPROM and 256K DRAM, and the Japanese government do the same on six other kinds of semi-conductors, including Japanese exports of semi-conductors to third countries; and
2. Japan set up an organization to expand its imports of semi-conductors from the United States and other countries.

This is a familiar story of protection and managed trade. The agreement would have been impossible if the Japanese Ministry of International Trade and Industry (MITI) had not used its influence to persuade Japanese producers to comply. The Japanese government wanted the cooperation of the US government on such matters as the stabilization of the yen and protectionist legislation in Congress. The monitoring agreement covers not only Japanese parent companies but their overseas subsidiaries elsewhere in Asia, thus effectively precluding the possibility of shipping from there to the United States. Second, it reflects the race that is going on in one of the most important high-technology industries. The pricing agreement will bring higher profits to Japanese producers for the moment, but it will also sharpen the competitive edge that South Korean producers have in the market for standard mass-produced memories. Third, it is a manifestation of deep US concerns about national security, since semi-conductors are widely used in high precision, high performance weapons as well as in civilian applications. The US government is worried that, if US domestic producers become steadily less competitive and the US chip market is occupied largely by foreign-based producers, US defence equipment will have no alternative but to rely on them. The decline of the domestic industrial basis for manufacturing weapons is seen as a grave problem for US national security.[2]

The intimate relationship between trade, technology and security is worth close examination, especially in the context of East Asia, one of the most dynamic regions in the world. Three characteristics of East Asia make this region an excellent case for the study of the interactions between trade, technology, and security. First, economic growth in East Asia is typically export-led; without smooth and large-scale trade flows, the East Asian economies cannot continue at their present levels of activity. Secondly, East Asia is continually seeking new and higher technologies; as a region it cannot compete without them because it is poor in resources. It is indicative of the importance attached to high technologies that the Japanese nickname for semi-conductors is 'the rice of industrial life'. Thirdly, the countries of East Asia are invariably plagued by a deep sense of vulnerability that drives them to seek desperately for security, to the extent of subordinating other national aspirations and priorities to that search.

The purpose of this chapter is twofold: first, to show that trade and technology issues can often give rise to sensitive questions of security; and second, to argue that prudent and balanced management of trade, technology and security is increasingly necessary in this region, which is so full of energy and dynamism yet marred by a significant degree of uncertainty and unpredictability. The rest of the chapter will deal with some of these issues under the following headings: protectionism in manufacturing sectors; the decline in the prices of primary commodities; the pressure towards liberalization; the increasing costliness of technological innovation; and security-inspired technological protectionism. The primary concern is with Japan and to a lesser extent, the two Pacific Newly Industrializing countries (NICs), South Korea and Taiwan, but also with China, the ASEAN countries and Australasia whenever it seems appropriate. This focus is justified because these three countries constitute a core component of the Western security system in East Asia and because they are the most dynamic countries in the region in terms of trade and technology.

Protectionism in manufacturing sectors

East Asia has its own rather heavy form of protectionism. A latecomer to industrialization normally has a wide array of regulations and protectionist policies designed to encourage indigenous industrialization. In order to obtain foreign currency reserves for the import of capital goods and technologies, agriculture (rice production) was heavily taxed in earlier periods,[3] but agriculture, especially rice and silk (which was one of the main primary export commodities) lost its competitive position as industrialization proceeded. This fact, together with high population density and poor natural resource endowment, has encouraged export-led industrialization that uses other markets of the world to the fullest extent to promote its own industrialization.

In those manufacturing sectors where the East Asian latecomers enjoy a competitive position – such as textiles, steel, chemicals, and certain electronic products – they are very aggressive in penetrating the markets of less competitive countries. In those sectors where the latecomers do not have a competitive edge, including electronics, telecommunications, software, and weapons, they try assiduously to protect their domestic market first. East Asia has enjoyed access to the huge US market for its exports for many years, but the US has been showing a steady decline in competitiveness in certain manufacturing sectors such as steel, chemicals, automobiles, textiles, machinery, and electric and electronic appliances. Protectionist measures are taken intermittently to provide emergency relief and time for adjustment. In 1984 US imports covered by special protection had a value of $US 68 billion, or 21 per cent of total imports.[4] What matters is that many of the goods and services covered by US special protection are from East Asia. In more than half of the 31 cases examined in the volume by Hufbauer *et al.* on the topic, the suppliers affected by special protection were primarily East Asian. Such cases were textiles and apparel (three cases), specialty steels, ball bearings, colour television receivers, CB (citizens' band) radios, bolts, nuts and large iron and steel screws, automobiles (three cases), heavyweight motorcycles, ceramic articles, book manufacturing, rubber footware, and canned tuna.

The intensification of trade disputes between East Asia and the United States is not always politically explosive, let alone security-related. In most cases, it simply means that East Asia has become much more competitive in certain sectors while the United States has become less so. However, it has longer-term security implications that cannot easily be dismissed. Since East Asia is dependent on trade flows to an unusual degree, what may be taken as 'improper' handling of East Asian countries by the United States can provoke nationalistic reactions from them. It is reasonable to conclude that the recent flare-up of Korean anti-Americanism took place against this background.[5] Though primarily directed against the South Korean government, the radical actions of students and workers seem increasingly to take on an anti-American character as well. Occupying US banks and cultural centres in Korea and committing suicide by self-immolation as a protest to the US and Korean governments are manifestations of the intensely political emotions of the Korean radicals. Nevertheless, the radicals aside, many Koreans seem to believe at the bottom of their hearts that South Korea, a front-line state which is shouldering heavy military burdens for the United States and the West in general, should be more or less exempt from US pressure over the regulation of exports of textiles and apparel, which is but a trifle compared with national security. This perception of the relationship that stresses its 'give-and-take' character could change the nature of alliance, with the erosion of what Koreans seem to believe is the 'take' side, namely the belief that the United States should take a lenient and generous position on Korea's management of its economy and trade.

The US way of dealing with trade issues certainly seems to irritate some Koreans. On the one hand, the United States encourages East Asians, as well as others, to become fully fledged members of the free trade system, and requests (or even pushes) Korea to liberalize trade, to deregulate financial institutions and to raise the value of the won against the dollar so that Korea's trade surplus with the United States will decrease. Yet this same United States virtually imposes on Korea – at least Koreans seem to feel that way – its protectionist measures in textiles and other products without the courtesy of 'proper' consultations with the governments of countries known for the value which they place on face-saving measures and rituals.[6] Similar considerations apply to other East Asian countries but South Korea represents the most acute case, the one where trade and security are linked most closely, if not quite directly. Since trade is a linchpin for the survival and prosperity of the East Asian countries, it can be argued that the aggravation of trade disputes, left to themselves, could encourage these countries to reconsider their security arrangements seriously over the longer term.[7] This is an important point that should be stressed because the economic, technological and military capabilities of these countries are steadily increasing.

From the other side of the Pacific, what Americans see as the intransigence of these countries tends to reduce the willingness of the United States to be ready to intervene effectively for their defense. Though public opinion about such willingness has been more or less stable for some years,[8] it is hardly necessary to state that in the longer term American public sentiment can be very volatile about its Asia policy. In other words, trade disputes have the potential to weaken the security ties across the Pacific substantially if they are not properly handled.

Decline of primary commodity prices

A recent study shows that throughout the world the amount of primary product required for a given unit of economic output has been shrinking by 1.25 per cent a year since 1900.[9] Since the production of primary commodities has been increasing very rapidly as a result of the heavy use of chemical fertilizers, extensive mechanization and other advances in agriculture and mining, prices have been basically on the decline over a long period. In the mid-1980s, the prices of raw materials recorded their lowest levels since the Second World War in relation to the prices of manufactured goods and services, and according to Peter Drucker this trend is not likely to be arrested for some time to come.[10] If that is the case, it is a grave matter for commodity-exporting countries. Half the exports of the Philippines, for example, are primary commodities.[11] It is thus no wonder that the Philippines, so heavily dependent on primary commodities for foreign exchange, has registered large current-account deficits, a problem further compounded by the borrowings from abroad for its industrialization efforts and the very high interest rates ruling during the first half of the 1980s in the United States and other countries. Needless to say, there are many more factors in the economic stagnation of the Philippines than the collapse of commodity prices, but there is no doubt that this is one of the main causes. As in the Korean case, the decline in the prices of raw materials is not directly related to security, but exports of raw materials do carry great weight in the Philippine economy and provide a large amount of government revenue which can be used for achieving stability and fostering a sense of national purpose. Economic stagnation and political instability are almost inevitable when industrialization programs do not progress faster and export earnings decline because of the collapse of primary commodities prices. Insurgency and instability obviously matter anyway, but the threat they pose to the two large and well-equipped US military bases in the Philippines concerns the security of the West in general.[12]

The decline of primary commodities trade affects not only the Philippines but also other resource-rich countries of the Asian-Pacific region, such as Malaysia, Indonesia, Australia, and New Zealand. The general dissatisfaction of those countries with large industrial economies such as the EC, Japan and the United States is clearly on the increase.[13] First, the industrial economies generally have a very high level of agricultural protection, which effectively prevents exporters of primary commodities from penetrating their markets. Among the East Asian countries, Japan, Korea, and Taiwan have the tightest protection of rice prices in the world.[14] Secondly, a large proportion of agricultural trade now takes place among the industrial countries of the North rather than between them and the commodity-exporting countries of the South. The commodity-exporting countries are harmed by bilateral and multilateral agricultural deals largely engineered by the industrial countries of the North, whether between the United States and the EC or between the United States and Japan. For example, the bilateral deal for beef between the United States and Japan has placed Australia at a disadvantage since lower-priced Australian beef could penetrate the Japanese market much more effectively, if that bilateral regulatory agreement did not exist.[15]

The prospect that the focus of the new round of GATT talks will include agriculture along with services, high technology and intellectual property does not excite most commodity-exporting countries, which were disappointed by the outcome of the Tokyo Round in agriculture.[16] There is general dissatisfaction on the part of raw material exporters with the closed European and Japanese agricultural markets, and with what seems to them to be the US attack on bilateral deals, using the US security leverage, which leaves them in an ever-worsening situation.[17] This widespread dissatisfaction is a powerful argument for devising a mechanism to ease the difficulties of commodity exporters in the region in the enlightened interest of the West.

Pressure towards liberalization

The western Pacific has become one of the most dynamic regions in the world, and is increasingly linked with the no less dynamic North American region in terms of trade, technology and finance flows.[18] It is no wonder that many people in the Pacific region have come to think that they would derive much benefit from the demolition of the large barriers across borders to trade, technology transfer and finance. Since the United States is the most powerful country in the region, its somewhat ambivalent strategy there merits special attention. The United States needs access to an increasingly large and dynamic market in the western Pacific, especially in those fields where the United States performs excellently but the regional states may not be so competitive – namely, agriculture, services and high technology. In turn, the regional countries need access to the US market (and that of Japan) for their exports of manufactured products.

Against this background, the United States has been following two tracks: multilateralism and bilateralism. The former is exhibited largely through the GATT trade talks and seeks the application of non-discriminatory free-trade principles, whereas the latter is manifested in bilateral negotiations toward free trade. What bothers some people in the western Pacific is the tendency of the United States to deal bilaterally with those regional countries where it can wield special influence in order to obtain concessions because of the security it provides.[19] Since liberalization is spearheaded by the United States, a country which was once hegemonic but now somewhat resigned to being *primus inter pares*, though reasserting itself through reshaping international rules,[20] countries that feel pushed into liberalization often manifest various forms of nationalistic reaction. The problem is real for those latecomers who have long adhered to traditions – norms, rules, and institutions – different from those of the early starters in Western Europe and North America. Japan and the Pacific NICs are such latecomers, broadly conceived. The question is whether these differences are manageable and how far the countries concerned can construct common rules.

One powerful argument for the necessity and desirability of such arrangements when there is severe conflict of interest has been put forward by Robert Keohane in a more general setting. He postulates that the US hegemony is over, and that co-ordination and cooperation with other states have become much more important than before in the maintenance of inter-national rules and institutions for the provision of what are called 'international public goods' or the international arrange-ments for peace and prosperity.[21] Keohane's specific prescription is a 'tit-for-tat' strategy to induce cooperation in a situation resembling the prisoner's dilemma. That is to say, when two actors do not cooperate they produce the worst collective out-come, but the outcome is still the second best for a defector – but the worst for a cooperator – unless both cooperate, when they produce the best outcome. In order not to have the worst collective outcome in repeated rounds of the game, Keohane, following Robert Axelrod,[22] suggests that non-cooperation should be punished but cooperation be rewarded. This strategy is presented as that of a *primus inter pares* after hegemony; the United States is still the greatest power, the one which takes the initiatives in an effort to exert its influence in reshaping inter-national institutions toward common goals. Whether the 'tit-for-tat' strategy is productive, especially in relation to the nature of strategy and the domestic foundations that can sustain the strategy of (presumably rational) state managers, must be empirically examined.

In the setting of trans-Pacific frictions, what is often observed, at least from the viewpoint of the Pacific NICs and Japan, is that the United States frequently resorts to request-cum-pressure, making full use of its security relationship with allies and part-ners in order to obtain further concessions from them in the forms of trade liberalization and financial deregulation.[23] Its strategy differs from one country to another: the most interest-ing case is perhaps that of South Korea where the United States has accumulated large trade deficits and is now pressing for further and faster liberalization. A slightly different example is Taiwan, which has accumulated a large surplus with the United States but has no security tie with it in the form of a security alliance. The US keeps pressing Taiwan for further trade liberalization, but in a somewhat milder fashion than with South Korea, although Taiwan does value the supply of weapons by Washington.

Of the three countries concerned, it is on Japan that the United States perhaps exerts the strongest pressure for further trade liberalization. This seems to be based on the (largely justifiable) view that Japan should play a far larger role than it does at present in reshaping international rules and bearing the burdens of international management in cooperation with the United States and other major countries.[24] Especially alarming to Japan's trade partners is its large current account surplus with them, including the US, the Pacific NICs and the members of ASEAN. For these countries, Japan represents the biggest problem among their trade issues. Their demands are basically threefold. First, that access to the Japanese market must be significantly increased. For that to happen, the various forms of regulation and protection applied by Japan in such matters as standards, distribution, employment, and subsidies must be drastically reduced. Secondly, that the Japanese economy must be reframed to encourage much higher levels of consumption; this should include tax reforms and moderation of the overdominant bureaucracy. Thirdly, that Japan should be more generous in its international contributions in such matters as security and technology transfer. Though Japan is participating more widely in what is sometimes called 'the provision of international public goods' (for example, Official Development Assistance (ODA) and contributions to international organizations), it is a little harder to do this in the fields of security and technology. First, the pacifist-isolationist impulse has been a strong disincentive to wider government involvement in international security arrangements: military technological cooperation is restricted to Japan's ally, the United States. Secondly, being a more advanced latecomer, Japan has until recently been much more hesitant and less generous than the United States about transferring technology to developing countries.

What bothers many Japanese is how the request-cum-pressure from the Americans is exerted. It is clear that many of the US demands are neither concerted nor coordinated within the United States. Rather, they are simply a manifestation of the pluralistic demands of the American political process. But from the Japanese viewpoint the US demands often give the impression that the United States wants to transform Japan by twisting its arm. Since history has made it quite clear that Japan is more than capable of adapting to a new politico-economic environment, it is perhaps unnecessary to stress that its flexibility would largely cancel out any potentially destabilizing effects of such pressures on the local economy. The point here, however, is the impact over the longer term of these interactions of pressure and response, demand and acquiescence, as reported in the Japanese press, on the psychological attitude of the Japanese.[25] Confronted with the always irresistible forces of what the Japanese call 'internationalization', many of them seem to be reverting to the values of traditional morality, the work ethic, and nationalism,[26] which may cause them to react unexpectedly to the three basic demands from abroad listed above.

What is more likely to become a perennial problem as Japan moves up the ladder of nations in economic, technological, and military capabilities is that two opposing forces will emerge in Japanese society: internationalism and isolationism. The higher the perceived short-term costs of cooperating and coordinating policies with the rest of the world, the more powerful the impulse to 'go it alone'. Depending on this balance, the directions that Japan might take could vary significantly. This is why political upheavals, small or large, in countries adjoining the United States are watched carefully in Japan. For instance, the US demand that Mexico scrap its nationalized industries, which form a linchpin of Mexico's ruling party, led to the resignation of its Finance Minister. In Canada, the prime minister's party has difficulty in pushing the 'go along with the US' policy in trade too far and too fast. South Korea's problems have already been discussed. For obvious reasons, these are developments that Japan cannot afford to overlook.

The increasing costliness of technological innovation

Technological innovation is always expensive for a forerunner. The costliness and uncertainties of technological advancement, coupled with the pervasiveness of technology in modern life, have made technology policy an area of very high priority for any government.[27] Furthermore, the fact that the United States has been widely acknowledged as a leader in many high-technology areas places the rest of the world in the difficult position of looking up to and following the US, while at the same time exploring areas where it can achieve something itself, albeit with high costs and uncertainties.

Japan has become more keenly aware of this difficulty as it has reached technological frontiers in a number of areas. The percentage of total revenue spent on R&D has risen steadily in many Japanese firms. The problem is that the United States, which used to be very generous to followers like Japan in disseminating technological information, has become much less so because it realizes that it is being overtaken by some of these followers. Especially in the high-technology areas, the US seems determined to retain its superiority.[28] Two main arguments seem to be salient in US demands on Japan.[29] One concerns reciprocity; the other security. The reciprocity argument is that, despite recent Japanese technological achievements, Japan is niggardly about disseminating its own technological information to other countries, and that without reciprocity the United States should deny Japan liberal access to American technology. The security argument is that Japan and some other countries are somewhat lax about making available some of the security-sensitive technologies to socialist countries, and so these technologies should not be given to Japan. The United States also seems to feel that Japan is not as forthcoming as it would like in making Japanese technological information available to it; thus the US Congress has recently passed a law intended to facilitate the translation of Japanese technological information into English.[30] There is a strong feeling in the United States that, if it is denied access to Japanese technological information, American universities and research institutions can legitimately stop the provision of such information to Japan. The reciprocity argument, of course, is often camouflaged by the security argument. In particular, the Act of 1985, which regulates exports of high-technology products and licences even to members of CoCom, effectively prohibits the dissemination of technologies even when they have been developed in US universities and research institutions under commissions from Japanese firms. The Act has recently been further revised to tighten the regulation, on the grounds that the Soviet Union obtains technological information from some Western countries.

The counter-argument (the liberal one) – that too much regulation of the dissemination of technological information will reduce the pace of US technological advance – is no less strong. The US government's regulation notwithstanding, US universities and research institutions have become increasingly dependent on collaboration with Japanese firms in financing research projects, as the US Federal Budget has become very tight. Against this practice not only security considerations but also concerns about competition are put forward; that is, that US–Japanese research collaboration facilitates the transfer of new technologies into manufacturing for Japanese firms, thus damaging US firms.

Japan's most likely course is to develop its two-track policy. One branch of this is to depart from the system of dependence on US research for technological information and to expand its niches on the technological frontiers autonomously, as far as it can; the other is to strengthen the Japan–US collaborative research system. Japan's choices in this respect will significantly affect the course it will take in terms of reframing its economy and restructuring its national security policy, and this is likely to be of great interest to the Western security system.

Security-inspired technological protectionism

The United States has intermittently manifested its strong protectionist impulse as many of its manufacturing sectors have become decreasingly competitive with Japan and some other countries. Pressure from these countries is such that as many as 200 protectionist bills have been tabled before Congress. In order to adhere to the overall principle of free trade, the President often accommodates some of the protectionist spirit in order to thwart protectionism. He vetoes outright protectionist bills while partially accommodating protectionist sentiments.[31]

One prominent example is the application of clause 232 of the Trade Enhancement Act, which purports to protect domestic industries for reasons of national security. Regulation of technology flows has become less effective since specialists have learned how to convert civil-use technology to military use without much difficulty. Given the inevitable diffusion of technology, the battle to move faster up the ladder of technological innovation is now fought much more fiercely. As domestic protectionist pressure mounts, its application has tended to widen. As far as Japan is concerned, the following five cases provide good illustrations:[32]

1. In February 1983 Kyoto Ceramics Inc. sold its subsidiary Dexel Inc. to Gould Inc. after it was advised to do so for security reasons.
2. In March 1983 President Reagan demanded voluntary export restraints on Japanese manufacturers of machinery until November 1986, when he was to make a decision on the application of clause 232 of the Trade Enhancement Act.
3. Mitsubishi Chemicals Inc. sold Optical Information Systems (a manufacturer of semi-conductors and laser instruments) to McDonnell Douglas Inc. at the request of the US Department of Defense (DOD) in December 1983.
4. Sumitomo Metallurgical Engineering, when purchasing Chase, Burns Inc., had to return the company's military division to Allegheny International at the 'request' of the Department of Defense in December 1983.
5. In September 1984 the Defense Department expressed concern about the purchase by Minnebear Inc. of New Hampshire Ballbearing Inc. and the matter is still in dispute.

There are four arguments relating to security-inspired technological protectionism. The first concerns security. In order to protect security-sensitive information, the argument runs, it is necessary to prevent firms that manufacture security-sensitive products from merging with, or being purchased by, foreign-based firms. If such mergers or purchases were allowed, security-sensitive products and technologies might be transferred to hostile foreign powers. This is actually the spirit of clause 232. The second concerns competition. In the US political system it is difficult to mobilize support without waving the banner of national security. Thus, even when it is simply a matter of reducing industrial and business competition, the national security argument can be used to justify prohibiting foreign firms from purchasing the manufacturers of security-sensitive products. The third is the technology argument. This claims that, even if dissemination of technological information and exports of sensitive products are forbidden, technology is bound to diffuse over the longer term because absolute geographical and communicational isolation does not exist. Even if isolation were possible, someone somewhere would probably come up with an idea leading to a technological breakthrough. In such a scenario, regulation might not matter too much either way. On balance, therefore, the negative effects of regulation on research achievements perhaps outweigh the positive ones in the longer run. The fourth argument is the liberal one, which goes as follows: under conditions where flows of trade and, by extension, flows of research communications are restricted, the global level of research advancement is likely to fall. Any hindrance to the freedom of research and communication is likely to produce goods that are less than satisfactory, and thus many countries will suffer from protectionism or autarchy in the longer run.

In the United States it is the first two arguments which have been strongly voiced recently, yet the technological imperatives also seem to be pushing in the direction of further collaboration with Japan. Japan therefore pursues, as noted earlier, a two-track policy: the autonomous development of technology side-by-side with close cooperative advancement with the United States.

The decision about whether and how to participate in the US SDI research program illustrates Japan's difficulties.[33] First, the Japanese government has had to take into account Japan's strongly pacifist bent, and the consequent legal and administrative commitments which constrain Japan's military and technological interaction with other countries. The first step towards participation in the program through a governmental agreement has already been taken; in line with the Japan–US Mutual Defense Assistance Agreement of 1954, the November 1983 Weapons Technology Exchange of Notes on the Provision of Weapons Technology to the US, and the December 1985 Exchange of Notes on Details of Implementation of the

November 1989 Exchange of Notes were concluded. The Japanese government has disarmed criticism by using the 1954 Agreement with the United States, and the two Exchanges-of-Notes have been concluded to adapt the Agreement to this particular case. Furthermore, the 1954 Agreement makes it easy to handle the implementation of the US demand for secrecy on certain matters, since it contains the appropriate clauses. Not surprisingly, it was only after the ruling Liberal Democratic Party's (LDP) resounding electoral victory on 6 July 1986 that the government announced (on 9 September 1986) its decision to participate in the programme through a formal agreement.[34]

Besides the problem of internal politics, the issue of technological costs and benefits must be considered. Many Japanese firms seem eager to be exposed to, and to benefit from, participation in parts of the SDI research program, and the trend toward US–Japanese collaboration appears to be further enhanced by Japan's willingness to participate. It is true that there is some apprehension over how to use the resulting technology products, but many firms seem to have calculated that the benefits will be greater than the costs in the longer term. The SDI program is seen – at least in the longer run – as opening up technological frontiers in many areas which will provide immense opportunities for Japanese industry. Government negotiations are under way about the problem of how to use the resulting technology products. It is yet to be seen, however, how successful the Japanese government will be in not accepting the formula contained in the agreement between the United States and West Germany, in which Germany's use of the products is severely circumscribed.

The security issue is seen basically in terms of Japanese co-operation with and contribution to the US-led security of the West. It is true that the Japanese government is no less concerned with the US–Soviet military balance, with the potential instability brought about by enhanced competition in ballistic missile defence (BMD) between the two superpowers, and with the effects that SDI may have on the numbers of ballistic missiles now deployed. But the view seems to be widely held in Japan that the SDI program will not create any immediate, tangible changes in the defense postures of the two superpowers or in the military balance. It is ironic that this view, coupled with the government's low-key and cautious attitude to the issue, has stifled any deepening of the discussion on Japan's participation in SDI research. The impact of BMD on Japanese security therefore, has been neither directly addressed nor widely discussed.

Four concerns seem to be common to America's allies. First, that US–Soviet competition over ballistic-missile offense and defense should not be allowed to increase military instability or the likelihood of a world war. Secondly, that US–Soviet competition should not work in the direction of subordinating considerations of national security to global security solely as perceived by the US government. Thirdly, that US–Soviet competition should not exclude US allies from the benefits of technological diffusion and spillover. Fourth, that US–Soviet competition should not be allowed to reduce the overall security of the West – including Japan. It seems that Japan and other East Asian countries are apprehensive about the general trend toward steady militarization in the region, but that most of them have not articulated their thoughts on BMD and the offensive stance that it may imply in so far as this affects their own security policies. China may be an exception to this observation. Being a nuclear power, China seems to be the most articulate about the SDI program and its probable consequences for its own security.[35] Not unnaturally, China is alarmed by the prospect of Soviet BMD.

On the more immediate issue of balanced cuts in the Intermediate-range Nuclear Forces (INF) deployed in Europe and Asia by the United States and the Soviet Union, both China and Japan are concerned that the US might not push the issue strongly enough with the Soviet Union, despite 'domestic political pressure, Soviet intransigence, and European insistence'.[36] Any US failure in this respect is likely to lead China to reconsider its strategy of using the United States as a counterweight to the Soviet Union. It is also likely to affect the embryonic large-scale defense cooperation between the United States and Japan. Japan has all along been less worried about Soviet INF than China, if only because of the belief that they are primarily targeted against China. Yet, if Japan becomes closely identified with US strategy, especially with its forward defense strategy, and if China distances itself further from the United States, the

Soviet Union might re-target some of its Asian INF from China to Japan. However, the new Soviet willingness to partake of what may be called Pacific economic dynamism with other Pacific countries, manifested in the Gorbachev speech at Vladivostok on 28 July 1986, might have some moderating effect on its policy toward Japan as well as China. South Korean developments should also be watched carefully in this regard. A recent publication of the 'Minutes of the Closed Hearings of a Subcommittee of the US House of Representatives' has shown that the US Air Force is planning to modernize nuclear munition stores in 26 US bases worldwide – including the US base at Kunsan, South Korea. This has brought a (somewhat disingenuous) statement from the South Korean government that it had not been informed of the plan. If it were implemented, it is perhaps possible that South Korea might reconsider its security policy.[37]

With respect to conventional weapons, the pacifist commitment of the Japanese government constrains the development of certain kinds of weapons. 'Offensive' weapons are not manufactured or imported and weapons manufactured by Japan cannot be exported. The government has even tended to discourage Japanese development of weapons. Thus half of the weapons of the Japanese Self-Defense Forces (SDF) are made in or licensed by the United States. Yet the impulse towards autonomy in the production of weapons has not been negligible, especially in the production of fighter aircraft. Although the SDF at present has only one kind of indigenously manufactured fighter, the F-1, the history of the development of the next ground-attack fighter, the FSX, is a manifestation of this impulse.[38] The final decision on the FSX appears to be that neither *Tornado* (built by three European countries), nor the F-18 (McDonnell Douglas), nor the F-16 (General Dynamics) satisfies the SDF. The three requirements the SDF sets for the FSX are that: 1) a support fighter should have some air defence capability as well as a capability against ground and maritime targets; 2) it should have two engines – for safety reasons; and 3) it should have a radius of action of 450 nautical miles (nm) when loaded with four air-to-sea missiles. Needless to say, two unstated criteria, national pride and the desire to develop indigenous technology, seem to be of the utmost importance in the decision. Not surprisingly therefore, 100 FSX fighter aircraft are to be manufactured by Mitsubishi Heavy Industries and other Japanese firms, with the participation of US engine manufacturers. The Japanese two-track policy on technology is evident here also.

Conclusion

Trade, technology and security are linked in the Pacific region, more so than some would like to think. They will remain linked because of East Asia's perennial sense of vulnerability and economic anxiety. Only if export-led growth, economies increasingly oriented towards high technology, and the restless search for security can be politically reconciled will the region remain stable. It is not clear that they can be reconciled satisfactorily for all parties because, as noted here, the elements of conflict undoubtedly exist and seem likely to remain unresolved. The problem is how to channel the region's undoubted energy in creative directions for the 'general good' of international security.

It could be argued that the East Asian countries, and more broadly the western Pacific countries, have basically set the direction of their economic development, and that what remains for them is simply to achieve political maturity and the consolidation of democratic politics.[39] It is true that political issues have come to loom large in East Asia, but it would be a mistake to think that the countries in the region have solved their economic problems for all time. Clearly they have not. Prudence and moderation are now needed more than ever, by all the actors across the Pacific, in dealing with these intricate issues.

Notes

1. Nihon Keizai Shimbun, 4 July 1986, 1 and 2 August 1986, *Far Eastern Economic Review,* 17 July 1986, p. 52; *The Economist,* 15–18 July 1986, pp. 53–4. See also special issues on high technology and high-technology trade, respectively, in *The Economist,* 23–9 August 1986, special pages 1–20 and Issues in *Science and Technology.* Vol. 2, No. 3 (Spring 1986), pp. 41–80.
2. Winston William, 'Japanese investment: a new worry', *New York*

Times, 6 May 1984, p. F1, *Electronic News,* 18 March 1986, p. 1,
cited in Ellen L. Frost, *For Richer, For Poorer: Managing Money, Technology and People in US–Japanese Relations,* pre-publication manuscript for the Council on Foreign Relations, Summer 1986. I am
grateful to Ellen Frost for making this available.

3. Kym Anderson and Yujiro Hayami, *The Political Economy of Agricultural Protection: East Asia in an International Perspective* (Sydney: Allen
& Unwin, 1986).

4. Gary Clyde Hufbauer *et al, Trade Practice in the United States: 31 Case
Studies* (Washington, DC: Institute for International Economics,
1986), p. 21. On US competitiveness, see Robert Z. Lawrence, *Can
America Compete?* (Washington, DC: The Brookings Institution,
1984).

5. *Far Eastern Economic Review,* 10 July 1986, pp. 36–41: *Asahi Shimbun,*
11 June 1986.

6. For 'Confucian propriety', see, for example, Lucian W. Pye, *Asian
Power and Politics* (Cambridge, MA.: Harvard University Press,
1985). In this connection, one telling event took place recently in
Korea: shortly before the US Secretary of State visited Korea to
meet the Korean foreign minister in early May 1986, the US
Special Security Team brought sniffer dogs into the building in an
attempt to detect explosives in the Foreign Minister's office and
the VIP lift without the sufficient prior understanding of the
Korean government. *Chungan Ilbo,* May 1986, cited in *Yomiuri
Shimbun,* 31 May 1986.

7. A similar view is found in Peter Polomka, *The Two Koreas: Catalyst
for Conflict in East Asia?,* Adelphi Paper 208 (London: IISS, 1986),
p. 37.

8. William Watts, *The United States and Japan: A Troubled Partnership*
(Cambridge, MA: Ballinger, 1984); *The United States and Asia:
Changing Attitudes and Politics* (Cambridge, MA: Lexington Books
1982).

9. David Sapsford, *Real Primary Commodities Prices: An Analysis of Long-
Run Movements,* IMF Internal Memorandum, 17 May 1986, cited
in Peter Drucker, 'The changed world economy', *Foreign Affairs,*
Vol. 64, No. 4 (Spring 1986), pp. 768–91.

10. *Ibid.;* World Bank, *World Development Report 1986,* Washington, DC:
World Bank, 1986.

11. World Bank, *World Bank Report 1986,* Washington, DC: World
Bank, 1986.

12. Research Institute for Peace and Security, *Asian Security 1985*
(Tokyo: RIPS, 1985).

13. Peter Drysdale, 'Japan's US-dependence syndrome as seen from
Australia', *Economics Today* (in Japanese), No. 1 (Spring 1986), pp.
96–103; and Drucker (*op. cit.* in note 9).

14. Anderson and Hayami (*op. cit.* in note 3).

15. Aurelia George, *The Politics of Australia–Japan Beef Trade: Current*

Issues, paper presented to the Australia, Asia and Agricultural Trade Issues Conference, Sydney, 18 June 1986.

16. Gary Clyde Hufbauer and Jeffrey Schott, *Trading for Growth: The Next Round of Trade Negotiations* (Cambridge, MA: MIT Press for Institute for International Economics, 1985), pp. 47-53; Drysdale (*op. cit.* in note 13).

17. 'Farm trade: seeds of war', *Far Eastern Economic Review*, 11 September 1986, pp. 138-63.

18. Hugh Patrick, 'The burgeoning American stake in the Pacific region', in James W. Morley (ed.), *The Pacific Basin: New Challenges for the United States* (New York: Academy of Political Science, 1986), pp. 59-75.

19. See, for example, Drysdale (*op. cit.* in note 13) although he does not include any discussion of security issues.

20. Robert Keohane, *After Hegemony: Cooperation and Discord in the World Political Economy* (Princeton, NJ: Princeton University Press, 1984). See also Robert O. Keohane and Joseph S. Nye, Jr, 'Two cheers for multilateralism', *Foreign Policy*, No. 60 (Fall 1985), pp. 148-67; Andrew Mack, 'The political economy of global decline: America in the 1980s', *Australian Outlook*, Vol. 40, No. 1 (April 1986), pp. 11-20; and Fred Halliday, *The Making of the New Cold War* (London: Verso, 1983).

21. Keohane (*op. cit.* in note 20).

22. Robert Axelrod, *The Evolution of Cooperation* (New York: Basic Books, 1981). For a fuller examination of Axelrod's theory, see Christopher J. Makins, 'The super-power's dilemma: negotiating in the nuclear age' in *Survival* July/August 1985, pp. 169-78.

23. This question is addressed briefly in my *Perspectives toward the Twentieth-First Century with Special Reference to the Western Pacific*, paper presented at the Annual Meeting of the International Studies Association, Anaheim, California, 26-9 March 1986.

24. This and other related issues are more fully discussed in my 'Japan's images and options: not a challenger, but a supporter', *Journal of Japanese Studies*, Vol. 12, No. 1 (1986), pp. 95-119, included as Chapter 2 of this volume, and 'The ideas and structures of foreign policy: Japan looking ahead with caution', in Takashi Inoguchi and Daniel Okimoto (eds), *The Changing International Context*, Vol. 2 of *The Political Economy of Japan*, Yasusuke Murakami and Hugh T. Patrick (general eds), (Stanford: Stanford University Press, 1988), pp. 23-63, 490-500. On US-Japan economic issues, see C. Fred Bergsten and William R. Cline, *The United States Japan Economic Problem* (Cambridge, MA: MIT Press for Institute for International Economics, 1985); Stephen Cohen. *Uneasy Partnership: Competition and Conflict in US-Japan Trade Disputes* (Baltimore, MD: Johns Hopkins University Press, 1985); Kiyohiko Fukushima, 'Japan's real trade policy', *Foreign Policy*, No. 59 (Summer 1985), pp. 22-39; Bernard Gordon, 'Truth in trading', *Foreign*

Policy, No. 61 (Winter 1985 6), pp. 94–108.

25. See Ellen L. Frost (*op. cit.* in note 2).
26. Takashi Inoguchi, 'The Japanese double election of July 6, 1986', *Electoral Studies,* Vol. 6, No. 1 (April 1987), pp. 63–9.
27. Anne G. Keatley (ed.), *Technological Frontiers and Foreign Relations* (Washington, DC: National Academy Press, 1985).
28. See Daniel Okimoto *et al* (eds), *Competitive Edge: The Semiconductor Industry in the US and Japan* (Stanford: Stanford University Press, 1984); and the two special issues in *The Economist* and *Issues in Science and Technology,* cited in note 1.
29. *Nikkei Sangyo Shimbun,* 24, 25, 26 June 1986.
30. *Nihon Keizai Shimbun* (evening edition), 24 June 1986.
31. 'Routing protectionism', *The Economist,* 9–15 August 1986, pp. 15–16.
32. *Mainichi Shimbun,* 24 May 1986.
33. On the SDI program and issues related to it, see Office for Technology Assessment, *Strategic Defense Initiatives* (Princeton NJ: Princeton University Press, 1986) and works listed therein. As for Japanese thinking, see for instance, *Tokyo Shimbun* (evening edition), 13 May 1986, *Nihon Keizai Shimbun,* 18 May 1986, *Asahi Shimbun* (evening edition), 1 May 1986. See also Daniel Sneider, 'Why does Japan avoid discussing its participation in the SDI program in terms of its own security issues?' *Asahi Journal* (in Japanese), 25 July 1986, pp. 9–13.
34. See, *The Asian Wall Street Journal,* 10 September 1986.
35. Banning Garrett and Bonnie Glaser, 'Chinese perspectives on the Strategic Defense Initiatives', *Problems of Communism,* March–April 1986, pp. 28–44.
36. Banning Garrett and Bonnie Glaser, 'Asia's stake in Moscow's missiles', *Far Eastern Economic Review,* 24 July 1986, pp. 42–3.
37. *Mainichi Shimbun,* 10 July 1986.
38. *Asahi Shimbun* (evening edition), 6 June 1986.
39. Richard Holbrooke, 'East Asia: the next challenge', *Foreign Affairs,* Vol. 64, No. 4 (Spring 1986), pp. 732–51.

5

Japan's politics of interdependence

This chapter describes and illustrates how Japan conceives the political meaning of many kinds of interdependence and uses this concept to advance what it considers to be its national interests and global interests without upsetting the balance of world interdependence. 'Interdependence' means the mutual vulnerability and sensitivity of all governing-cum-economic units in the world.[1] 'The politics of interdependence' means, then, how actors make strategic use of interdependence with enough self-restraint not to jeopardize the system of interdependence itself.[2] Thus 'Japan's politics of interdependence' means how Japan makes strategic use of interdependence guided by its own standards of conduct. In this sense, this chapter is an attempt to combine the following two intellectual traditions: the interdependence literature[3] and the economic statecraft literature[4] to define Japan's politics of interdependence.[5] First, I will summarize three principles of Japan's political conceptualization of interdependence. Then I will illustrate them by some recent examples. Thirdly, prospects for Japan's politics of interdependence will be briefly discussed along with some discussion on the lines of research to be further explored.

Japan's politics of interdependence

Internally generated strength as source of power

In order for interdependence to function without bringing about excessive vicissitudes in the system as a whole, each participating unit needs to be equipped with internally generated strength. Needless to say, not all the participating units enjoy sufficient internal strength. As interdependence requires all the constituting units to interact with each other with inevitable pressure toward intermittent structural adjustments, the ability of each participating unit to cope with structural adjustments must be central to any discussion on the politics of interdependence. Not only the external economic policy but also the *internal* economic policy must be taken into account in any discussion of the politics of interdependence.[6] This principle is salient to Japan's politics of interdependence because of the country's history.

Looking back to Japan's national development, one cannot help but be impressed by how tenaciously Japan sought to overcome what it regarded as unequal treatment in the world.[7] Two most visible and symbolic experiences were extraterritoriality and lack of tariff autonomy, which had been imposed on Japan in the mid-nineteenth century when it was forced to open the country after two-and-a-half centuries of self-imposed isolation from the rest of the world. It is not an exaggeration to say that one major driving force of nineteenth-century modernizing Japan was to become the master of its own people, territory, and economy. Having been forced by gunboats to conclude unequal treaties, Japan was eager to establish its self-reliance, political, economic, and military. These efforts were to bear fruit gradually as its nation-building proceeded. Extraterritoriality was terminated toward the end of the nineteenth century. Tariff autonomy was recovered in the first decade of the twentieth century.

More fundamentally, Japanese leaders developed their *idée fixe* in the nineteenth century to the effect that the world is a competitive place where, unless well guarded and well prepared to meet whatever challenges may come, one can be easily and mercilessly victimized. Such was the thought of many Japanese leaders when they saw the comparative development in the nineteenth century and into the twentieth century of Vietnam, Korea, and China on the one hand and Japan on the other. In order not to succumb to the bitter fate of these three neighbors, Japan was to build and advance its own internally generated strength. The subsequent experiences in the twentieth century, especially during the war and thereafter, seemed only to re-inforce Japanese belief in the need for building internal strength. Needless to say, in addition to the external stimuli from international relations and the world markets, a number of internal factors helped to sustain this developmental strategy in the long term. They are first, high educational standards and a highly trained labor force; secondly, a strong sense of national-ism and loyalty and devotion to one's organization, and thirdly, relatively strong egalitarianism and collectivism.

The need for internally generated strength as a precondition for healthy interdependence is recognized time and again whenever Japan experiences externally derived economic dis-turbances. The economic blockade of the 1930s and 1940s and the discrimination against Japan until its accession to the GATT in 1955 are still well remembered. Also the US embargo on soya beans to Japan and the Arab embargo on petroleum in the early 1970s revived memories of such experiences.

Market forces take command

One's determination to be self-reliant is not necessarily the key to success, even when some internal factors help to sustain such a determination. The second principle of Japan's politics of interdependence is to let market forces take command. Unlike Mao Zedong, the Japanese have not allowed politics to take command in the long term because no political strategy can succeed against market forces. In other words, as long as inter-dependence is the system based on market forces, Japan should not swim against it in the longer term. It should swim in the same direction as the world market.[8] In the shorter term Japan might be able to swim against it. Or it might be able to turn the tide of the world market somewhat in the shorter term. Yet Japan's politics of interdependence seems to rest in the belief that policies matter only at the margin – if it is a fairly wide one – and have temporary limited effectiveness. Rather more critical importance is attached to intelligence about and analysis of the world market at macro- and micro-levels and relating them to the policy action that should or should not be adopted. Here I am talking about both national policy-makers and business managers. Not only the latter but also the former are aware of the primordial importance of this principle in playing the politics of interdependence, whether they are interested in protecting domestic political coalition patterns by temporarily limiting market liberalization or making use of foreign pressure in precipitating domestic political realignment; or whether they are interested in enhancing Japan's freedom of movement by creating and making use of the web of interdependence with the rest of the world; or whether they are interested in not asserting themselves too much in their concern not to disturb and disrupt the otherwise well-functioning web of interdependence.[9]

This belief does not seem to have changed very much even since Japan became an economic superpower. Two things should be distinguished here. One· is the small-country assumption whereby a small country benefits most when it acts according to the principle that its action does not have much effect on the rest of the world, whereas the action of the rest of the world makes an enormous difference to a small country. The other is the self-restraint on the part of a large country in not creating unnecessary disruptions to the web of interdependence by its own ill-conceived, often selfish and somewhat arbitrary policy. Even if Japan is a large country, it is also a country with a vested interest in the smooth functioning of the world economy as a whole, since its interests are so closely tied to the stability and prosperity of the world economic system. It is a country which is much more strongly constrained than some observers might expect by the apprehension that unless the web of interdependence is kept healthy and prosperous, Japan's future could become more uncertain and its position even untenable. That is why such words as caution, prudence and balance are more often heard from Japan than is normally expected of a large country with limited dependence on the rest of the world.

Since Japan is now in a position to affect the economy of the rest of the world not inconsiderably,[10] such a statement might provoke skepticism. Yet the second principle of Japan's politics of interdependence is not to exaggerate the power of policy on the world market. Its policy efforts at generating and sustaining its own internal strength are, however, somewhat different. This is why some see Japan's politics of interdependence as aiming primarily to generate competitive strength.[11] Yet one should not be misled by that notion into the belief that Japan's politics of interdependence always prescribes swimming against comparative advantage. Rather, the picture that emerges from a meticulous statistical analysis of comparative advantage and structural adaptation[12] points to the conclusion that Japan swims with comparative advantage. To transform comparative disadvantage into competitive advantage needs a whole range of good intelligence about markets, overall national welfare assessment of the industrial sector concerned, and administrative capability to execute policies with continuity and improvised adaptability.[13]

Government as provider of information and incentives to private actors

The government plays certain important roles. The third principle of Japan's politics of interdependence is the government's role in providing information and incentives to private actors. After all, the most the government can hope for *vis-à-vis* private actors is to guide them by providing them with good economic and policy intelligence and by motivating them to act in the way the government wishes by persuading them that they would benefit from so doing in the long run.[14] Needless to say, the government may at times have a number of administrative and non-administrative tools at its command. But its continuous effectiveness is not just dependent on the government's overall power of regulation, permission, and subsidies. It is also critically dependent on the right advice on market direction and policy relevance by means of incentives. For instance, if the government wants private actors to place more direct investment in a particular area or country where risks are generally considered to be high, the government might, for instance, legislate a policy package to which risk-absorbing insurance schemes are attached, and offer firms free access to a host of local investment-related data.

As interdependence relies so much on private actors playing the game according to their imperatives on profits, market shares, and employment, the government must come up with the schemes to orchestrate private actors' efforts so as to satisfy them and also achieve the general policy goals of the government. That is why the third principle is of crucial importance.

Interdependence deals not so much with high politics where the government is its own formulator and implementor of policy action, as with low politics where private actors are their own helmsmen. This partly explains why the politics of interdependence tends to be reactive rather than proactive in many cases, since the government often has to consult private actors and, no less important, to watch and assess the direction of market forces before it makes its decision. Since Japan's foreign policy is concerned with low politics or the politics of interdependence to an unusually high degree, Japan is often characterized as the reactive state.[15] Needless to say, in addition to this may be cited such factors as Japan's low-profile diplomatic tradition throughout most of the post-war years and the slow-moving formation of a consensus at home.

In spite of such a policy, the government can blunder at times. Some commentators even assert that the government's failure to act as a credible scheme-provider has in fact contributed to the better-functioning of market forces.[16] After all, no government is infallible or of boundless foresight. Yet, one must also add that the Japanese government has often behaved more decisively and effectively *vis-à-vis* private actors than some other governments.

Three examples

The three basic principles guiding Japan's politics of interdependence are revealed in some recent examples.

China

Japan's suspension of its official development assistance to China shortly after the Tiananmen Square massacre of protesters in June 1989 is understood better in the light of the gradually deepening economic interdependence between the two countries since the conclusion of the Peace and Friendship Treaty in 1978.[17] Both sides have every reason to enhance economic ties. First, China has a legitimate claim on Japan to receive every possible kind of help in its ambitious modernization programme in the light of Japan's historical debt to China. China has reinforced its argument by abandoning its claim for war indemnities from Japan. China believes it deserves the best treatment from Japan of all the countries in the world because of the debt of history.[18] Secondly, Japan wants to see a stable and friendly China. Japan's help in China's modernization is expected to have some effect in that respect. Given the difficulties Japan has *vis-à-vis* the United States (because of increasing competition) and the Soviet Union (because of territories and general relationship), China's stability and friendship are deemed essential for Japan to navigate the sea of rapid change toward the twenty-first century. Thirdly, Japan's private sector wants to see China develop as a good market in the long term. The myth of the China market has been held by many Westerners and Japanese for centuries. The Japanese are no exception to this. Although their initial optimism was shattered very fast by 1980–1, when China's economic trouble forced it to terminate many projects with foreign participation abruptly, Japanese private sectors have been alert to economic intelligence in the hope that one day China will become a good market as a result of the gradually permeating Pacific dynamism[19] in which China's coastal provinces are increasingly sharing.[20]

Fourthly, China's modernization needs Japan's economic, technological and financial help. What China needs for successful modernization includes many things in which Japan can be of help.[21] 1) Japan is China's number-one trade partner. Japan's export of machinery and other intermediate products is essential to Chinese manufacturing firms. The proportion of China's import of these goods from Japan has been very high. China's exports to Japan are essential for China to accumulate foreign reserves. Its exports consist largely of petroleum and its products and more recently of light manufactured products. 2) Japan's large-scale yen loan packages are indispensable to the Chinese government to consolidate its investments in economic and social infrastructures. The third package to be completed for the period between 1990 and 1995 is one of those which were suspended in 1989. In that year, the Chinese central government revenue was dependent on foreign loans by 4 per cent. More than two-thirds of these were from Japan.[22] With these

suspended and with much tax revenue going to local government and local firms rather than to the central government
because of its decentralization-oriented reform policy, the central government had a hard time. 3) Japan's direct investment
and associated technology transfer is essential to China's development. Japan's direct investment has been somewhat cautious
in general compared to its trade relationship and its official
development assistance. Japanese business firms are deterred
by inadequacies in the business climate in terms of energy supply, transportation, communication, supply of parts, regulation
of domestic sales of products, difficulty of changing profits into
foreign currencies, and difficulty of hiring people according to
the preferences of Japanese management leaders. Thus Japan's
direct investment in China accounts for only around 1 per cent
of total Japanese direct investment throughout the rest of the
world. Yet Japan's direct investment in China has been second
for many years after Hong Kong's. More recently, because of
Japan's economic sanctions and because of Taiwan's assiduously pursued economic interactions with China, Taiwan's
direct investment in China has been increasing very fast.

Given the background to Japan's post-Tiananmen China
policy, its course is easy to understand. First, Japan does not
want to alienate or isolate China from the rest of the world
including Japan itself. Thus Japan's protest to the Chinese
government was strong but brief and carefully phrased, somewhat different in tone from those of most Western governments. Secondly, Japan demonstrated its policy not to support
any governments which were too oppressive or aggressive in
part to dispel the oft-held image of Japan as doing business as
usual and in part to show its strong commitment to such values
as freedom and democracy in common with other industrial
democracies. For example, Japan suspended its ODA (Official
Development Assistance) to Vietnam in 1979 shortly after Vietnam's aggression in Cambodia; this suspension has continued
to the present except for humanitarian aids. Furthermore,
Japan is not unaware of the danger of disagreement with Western countries on China, which is widely thought to have been
one of the major causes of war in the 1940s.

Thirdly, Japan is apparently conscious of the effect of sanctions on the Chinese government. This is where Japan's politics

of interdependence comes in. As mentioned earlier, Japan's suspension of government loans has hit China's central government very severely. It is easy to understand that Chinese planners had immense difficulties with the national budget. With renewed economic tightening and replanning some areas of the economy, the central government has been trying to overcome its difficulties. Yet Prime Minister Li Peng could not help but express his complaint during autumn 1989 to one Japanese business delegation to the effect that while Western countries criticized China harshly on the Tiananmen incident but carried on business as usual, the Japanese government criticized China less harshly but Japanese business had dwindled significantly. Li Peng pleaded that 100 million people should not be starved by continuing the suspension.[23] Japan seems to be aware of its stronger position *vis-à-vis* China since the Tiananmen Square incident. The Japanese posture had been somewhat defensive until then because of its debt of history. China on the other hand was somewhat more active, exploiting the Japanese debt of history, in eliciting more aid, trade, and technology and even leading one deputy foreign minister to resign for his comment on Deng Xiaoping, who was said to be 'above the clouds'. The meaning was taken by Deng as alluding to his old age and his inability to keep up with current affairs.[24] Although there is no sign that the debt of history issue has subsided since June 1989, Japan seems to have increased its bargaining position *vis-à-vis* China on the basis of China's dependence on Japan's help. The result is an ironical twist of historical forces working between the two: namely, Japan's past misconduct creating its debt of history to China, which in turn led China to exploit it to its own advantage especially for its modernization efforts, which in turn has created the strong web of interdependence and has led China to curtail somewhat its erstwhile much harsher criticism of Japan's debt of history.

At the Western summit in Houston in July 1990, the Japanese government announced its plan to resume its ODA to China despite some opposition to it among the participants. A number of factors led to the decision. First, Japan does not want to see China suffer from long-term isolation and instability. Secondly, the United States has been ameliorating its policy toward China to a certain extent as exemplified by its decision on the one-year extension of the most favored nation clause to China. The departure of Fang Lizhi and his wife, dissidents who sought asylum at the US Embassy at Peking after June 4, 1989, first to the United Kingdom and then perhaps to the United States with a pledge to the Chinese government not to get involved in politics, is a further example. Thirdly, Japan seems to recognise that the prolongation of sanctions is harmful to the healthy interdependence of the two countries. If Japan is seen as exploiting China's vulnerability, then this will reinforce Japan's negative image as a ruthless exploiter of economic weakness. That would not be advantageous to Japan in the long term.

These results should not all be attributed to the skilful economic statecraft of the Japanese government in an era of interdependence. But three principles should be identified. First, the Japanese belief in the need for self-strengthening is exemplified in a preponderance of loans over grants. In their view, giving grants in too large an amount spoils recipients.[25] If they cannot manage loan repayments by industrializing the economy rapidly and thus generating enough surplus through self-discipline, then self-strengthening will not be achieved. Secondly, the Japanese government's belief in market forces seems vindicated by increasing economic interdependence created by mutual needs and the historical legacy, creating what appears to be a basis for peaceful and stable relations. Thus the Japanese government does not try to swim against the current of the world market. Even if China believes that China should receive the largest share of Japanese direct investment, the Japanese government leaves business decisions largely to the private sector. Thirdly, the Japanese government is adept at using incentives to the private sector in the form of creating the markets for financing and manufacturing firms through official development assistance. It can also bring about a more favorable environment for the private sector's direct investment by concluding the investment protection agreement with the Chinese government. By such an agreement what is called the 'national treatment' of Japanese direct investment is guaranteed.

The United States

Japan and the United States, the two largest economies in the world, have built an unprecedented degree of interdependence. Yet their interdependence has been beset by many problems.[26] One of the perennial issues impeding further consolidation of their interdependence is trade, and there are other economic issues too. The Structural Impediments Initiative (SII) Talks between Japan and the United States resulted in an accord in June 1990 designed to rectify those trade barriers which are alleged to hinder foreign products and firms from penetrating the Japanese markets. The accord obliges Japan to do a number of things, which include: (a) gearing up public works expenditure over the next decade; (b) moderating a number of regulations on setting up big stores; (c) enhancing implementation of the Anti-Monopoly Law. They are considered by the United States government as positive both in terms of accelerating Japan's market liberalization and as a means of reducing US trade deficits *vis-à-vis* Japan. The questions arise why the US government acted as if it were a Japanese opposition party with consumer-oriented policy preferences trying to press the Japanese government to remedy more vigorously some deficiencies in Japanese market liberalization, and why the Japanese government allowed the US government to engage in what might otherwise be considered as interference in domestic affairs.

First, the United States has long demanded more vigorous market liberalization by Japan,[27] which has been liberalizing its markets quite steadily, especially since the publication of the Maekawa Report in 1986. For the past four years Japan's imports have doubled in total volume partly because of renewed liberalization. Yet the US trade deficit *vis-à-vis* Japan has not changed much, although Japan's trade surplus has been dwindling very steadily – almost down to half of the previous year's level in winter 1990. Yet, not seeing any tangible reduction of its own trade deficit *vis-à-vis* Japan, the United States wanted to remedy further some alleged non-tariff barriers since most tariff barriers for manufactured and other products have been removed, making Japan the most thoroughly liberalized of all OECD countries. Since the US government faces a Congress very critical of its handling of trade deficit issues *vis-à-vis* Japan, it is thus forced to act vigorously in this respect while not jeopardizing overall the friendship between the two countries.

Secondly, the Japanese government wants to accommodate the US government's demands on structural impediments as much as possible since Japan needs the continuing friendship with the United States.[28] Yet the domestic opposition to those demands abound, especially within the government itself. Those ministries with vested interests in regulation of stores and monopoly on budgeting have resisted hard. Those private sectors most likely to be damaged if such demands are to be fully implemented have resisted no less vigorously. Thus prior to the SII spring talks of 1990, much had to be done in terms of 'massaging' the domestic resistance. The very 'backward' opposition of ministries had to be softened by a series of actions such as meetings and telephone calls on the part of high-ranking politicians including Prime Minister Toshiki Kaifu, President George Bush, Noboru Takeshita, a former prime minister, and Shin Kanemaru, former Deputy Prime Minister. They were concerned about a possible adverse effect on Japan–US relations by accommodating US demands only grudgingly and too late. The concern was shared by three actors in Japan: Prime Minister Kaifu whose power base was so weak that he had to rely more on the support of public opinion and diplomatic saliency; the Takeshita faction, the largest faction within the governing party, which has had to act behind prime ministers who are from very minor factions (it has held the prime ministership only twice between 1972 and 1990 – from 1972–4 and from 1987–9 – while between 1955 and 1972 the largest faction produced most prime ministers except for two months in 1957 and 1958);[29] and the Ministry of Foreign Affairs, whose power base is weak at home and which has to rely on the prime minister's authority to win over domestic agencies.[30]

Both the US and Japanese governments, especially the Foreign Ministry and the State Department, were very eager to keep things moving forward, because of strong opposition at home to what are considered to be humiliatingly conciliatory gestures to the adversary. After all, both Japan-bashers and US-bashers represent an important fraction of the strong opposition to these two governments. However, these two governments believe that the robust interdependent relationship of the two countries is to be one of the cornerstones in managing the world economy and that most other matters have lower priority.

Japan's politics of interdependence is applied to Japan–US relations most saliently. First, Japan wants to rely on internally generated strength, departing from its overdependence on the United States, which was deemed to be excessive especially during the decade beginning in the mid-1970s. The most dramatic realization toward that goal was a steady increase of domestic demand in total GNP. Export dependency has been on the steady decline for the latter half of the 1980s, while for the decade between the mid-1970s and the mid-1980s the figure was unusually high even in comparison with those figures in the 1950s and 1960s. The higher petroleum prices and the tighter fiscal policy during the decade made Japan's reliance on exports extraordinary and extreme. Yet what is becoming increasingly clear is that with the steady expansion of domestic demand, Japan's dependence on imports has been decreasing very steadily (6.3 per cent of GNP). What is worthy of note is that the comparable figure for the United States is 9.4 per cent and that the United States' dependence on the rest of the world has been on the steady rise. In other words, if the import/GNP ratio be taken as the indicator which allows one to count the United States as a continental economy, then Japan is a quasi-continental economy. The expansion of domestic demand has been achieved in part because Japan wanted to rely less on exports and less on the United States in order to make Japan–US interdependence more balanced and healthy.

Secondly, Japan wants to swim with world market forces. Since market liberalization has been the major current of the world economy, this is understandable. Besides, Japan has every reason to do so for internal reasons as well, since a highly regulated economy does not fit the status of a most advanced country. Japan's market-conforming behavior is very clear when one looks at structural adjustments since 1973. The first oil crisis hit Japan hard. Against all the prophets of that time at home and abroad, pointing to the imminent collapse of the Japanese economy without its own internal petroleum supply, Japan emerged strong by 1975 by remarkably trimming energy consumption in manufacturing and transportation. What was

called the 'high yen revolution' during the first Reagan presidency, whereby the deliberately cheaper dollar policy was pursued by the United States, made many Japanese apprehensive
about whether manufacturing firms could cope with the high
yen exchange rate when the world economy was in deep recession and the Japanese economy was more dependent than
usual on exports. Yet not only Japanese firms achieved an
enormous degree of efficiency in terms of trimming all kinds of
costs but the Japanese economy as a whole also completed
structural adjustments fairly smoothly. Amid the booming of
domestic demand during the latter half of the 1980s and into
the 1990s, came the demand for restructuring economic and
social institutions in the form of sector-specific talks and talks
about structural impediments initiatives. These forces have
been acting an an impetus for Japan to reexamine those somewhat outmoded and yet politically retained institutions, especially
in conjunction with the efforts at political reforms including the
electoral system and party funding. It looks as if the SII talks
will have some beneficial results for Japanese consumers to a
certain extent, while their effects on US trade deficits will
remain a moot question.

The point here is that Japan swims with the tide, not against
it. By so doing Japan has been able to adapt, on the whole quite
adroitly, to the dauntingly rapid structural changes in the world
markets. Although the Japanese government has often been
described as 'the reactive state' in foreign economic policy formation,[31] it is often vindicated since the government has to consult private actors who must take all responsibility for their
decisions by themselves, irrespective of the government's
wishes and requests. Thus even though the Japanese government at times seems slow in making its foreign economic policy
decisions, the Japanese economy as a whole has been most successful in swimming with the tide of the world market, because
private business firms have been assiduous in assessing the
markets and making their decisions. The politics of interdependence seems to rest more on balance and caution in market
behavior than on thrust and boldness in political leadership.

Thirdly, the Japanese government has been relatively skilful
in using its own power to influence private actors in the direction
in which it likes to see them move. Thus, when foreign criticism

of Japanese export-led growth and Japanese trade surplus mounted during the late 1970s and mid-1980s, the Japanese government got ready to import more from abroad through what might be called suggestive administrative guidance. It was active in doing this by providing information on products and suggesting some targets, related to the percentage of imports over all the parts they use in manufacturing, to be achieved by each firm. Although it is not quite clear whether the increase in Japanese imports has been achieved largely on account of the government's exhortation of private actors, the government does play a positive role in this way. The amount of imports doubled between 1985 and 1989. With the rise of the Japanese yen *vis-à-vis* the US dollar, its own domestic demand increased its weight very steadily. Furthermore, the Japanese government showed its benign neglect of the steeply rising price of land in Tokyo, thus helping many land-holding firms to get an immense amount of profit and thus enhance their financial position globally. The capital surplus thus accumulated and the high exchange rate of the Japanese yen, in addition to the need to allay foreign criticism of the accumulating trade surplus, have encouraged many Japanese firms to place a large amount of capital in foreign direct and portfolio investment, especially in the United States. Furthermore, Japanese institutional investors have found it profitable to purchase Treasury bonds, thus enhancing the US government's dependence on Japan and partially offsetting Japan's over-reliance on the United States in trade, technology, and security.[32] At the same time, the Japanese government and firms tried hard to diversify their export markets throughout the world. Japanese trade, aid, investment and financial networks have helped other Pacific Asian economies to grow and the balance has shifted accordingly in favor of Pacific Asia.[33] The Japanese government has been trying hard to encourage firms to move into the European Economic Community before a higher wall is built toward 1992.[34]

Eastern Europe

In January 1990 Prime Minister Toshiki Kaifu visited two East European capitals, Warsaw and Budapest, pledging Japan's loan package to Eastern Europe which has been trying to replace its old command economies by more market-oriented economies. The package is an ingenious one in a number of senses.[35] First, Japan wants to increase its say in European affairs. In an era of global interdependence Japan, having economic stakes in virtually every corner of the world, cannot afford to sacrifice global interests in favor of geographically narrow regional interests. No regionalist orientation would work. Japan's globalist orientation could not possibly leave Europe untouched by Japan. Japan's aid to Eastern Europe would help it to trade with Europe more vigorously. It is important especially in light of the still pervasive image of Japan as a selfish free rider and in view of the dictum, 'a friend in need is a friend indeed'.

Eastern Europe is facing all kinds of economic shortage. Japan's economic vigor and its anti-Russian (anti-Soviet) and non-colonial past in the region seem to make Japan a very popular nation in some of the East European countries. For instance, in Poland Japan is ranked at the top of all nations in the world in terms of its favourable image.[36] Western Europe is preoccupied with its own affairs, looking toward 1992 and further and is not particularly well-endowed financially especially as a reunifying Germany is preoccupied with its own financial problems. The newly-created European Development Bank is said to be thinking about Japanese contributions, if not its voice or vote. The United States has been concerned about its trade and government deficits which are of monstrous proportions.

Secondly, Japan's economic presence might make it easier for Japan to improve its relations with a further integrated European Community toward 1992. When Eastern European countries want to strengthen their ties with the European Community and when East Germany becomes a member of the Community, it might turn out to be a very good strategy. Thirdly, enhanced ties with East European countries might lead the Soviet Union by example to developing closer economic ties with Japan. Japanese assistance in Eastern Europe seems to be reducing the Soviet suspicion of Japan. As a matter of fact, the Soviet Union has been moving in the direction of receiving economic assistance from European countries and suggesting to Japan the kind of scheme that was applied to China in 1978, namely, the extension of large-scale economic assistance and participation in order not to destabilize the country further. The Western summit at Houston in July 1990 has made it clear that continental Europeans are eager to assist the Soviet Union financially and otherwise whereas others, namely, Japan, the United States, the United Kingdom and Canada offer what is called 'intellectual and technical assistance' to it, but not financial aid. Fourthly, Japanese economic participation in Eastern European countries will help to moderate German economic predominance in the region. Already the Japanese are the second largest lender to Eastern Europe, after West Germany.

One of the advantages of this loan package is that the government pledges to insure companies against loss incurred by venturing into the region, but unless firms move into the region, either with direct investment or loans, no great expenditure is necessary. The government seems to foresee that Japanese firms will not go there in large numbers anyway, given the extraordinary range of difficulties in restructuring the economies.[37] It also squares with the Japanese belief that not much trust can be placed in the effectiveness of grants in generating sustained economic development. According to that belief, local economies should be able to produce more surplus than just sufficient to continue to service debts. Thus the design of the package is such as to make it largely dependent on market forces functioning in the local economies as well as in the Japanese economy. Yet the pledging of the loan package is not only a political plus to Japan. But also in the longer term it is beyond doubt that some Japanese business firms will find and develop their business there. Given the small size of GNP in the region, any Japanese economic participation even of small size by Japanese standards will make a fairly large impact on the local economies.

Conclusion

This chapter has argued that the three principles guiding Japan's politics of interdependence are: the Japanese willingness to rely on internally generated strength which is of historical origin; the Japanese belief in market forces determining a large percentage of the outcome of interdependence and thus not exaggerating the power of policy in altering market forces, which can come only via internally generated strength; and the Japanese government's skill in motivating private actors to move in the direction the government prefers by giving information and incentives to them. The three principles have been illustrated if very briefly by the three examples: China, the United States, and Eastern Europe. My discussion on the three principles seems to suggest that in order better to understand Japan's politics of interdependence, at least three kinds of literature have to be further examined. First is the history of economic thought governing Japanese industrialization and modernization. Japan's economic experiences seem to provide a good example of the indigenous developmental model, or an antidote to the dependency model.[38] The second is the theory and practice of interdependence. The strategic aspect of interdependence especially must be further explored.[39] The third is the theory and practice of public policy or government–business relationship.[40]

Then, what are the prospects for Japan's politics of interdependence? In order to see them better, it will be useful to examine the prospect for each of the three guiding principles, if briefly. First, Japan's preference for relying on internal strength will become more salient as its own economic strength increases. Secondly, Japan's adroit use of market forces by swimming with the current will not change much unless Japan overestimates its own political power. Thirdly, the Japanese government's ability to influence private actors at home will decline somewhat as the private sectors become increasingly stronger *vis-à-vis* the government. To sum up, Japan's politics of interdependence will not change very much in the 1990s. But the combination of growing economic strength, its possibly already developing hubris, and its declining grip on the private sector may augur ill for its successful performance into the 1990s and beyond.

Notes

1. Robert O. Keohane and Joseph S. Nye, Jr, *Power and Interdependence* (Boston, Mass.: Little, Brown & Co., 1977).
2 G. Ionescu, 'On the development of both democracy and political

science under the impact of interdependence', paper presented at conference on 'Democracy and the Development of Political Science', Barcelona, 15–18 May 1990.

3. Richard Cooper, *The Economics of Interdependence* (New York: Free Press, 1968); Keohane and Nye, *op. cit.*; Peter Drysdale, *International Economic Pluralism: Economic Policy in East Asia and the Pacific* (Sydney: Allen & Unwin, 1988).

4. Jacob Viner, 'Power versus plenty as objectives of foreign policy in the seventeenth and eighteenth centuries', *World Politics*, Vol. I, October 1948, pp.1–29; Stephen Krasner, *Defending the National Interest* (Princeton: Princeton University Press, 1976); Peter J. Katzentstein (ed.), *Between Power and Plenty* (Madison: University of Wisconsin Press, 1978); David Baldwin, *Economic Statecraft* (Princeton, NJ: Princeton University Press, 1985); Richard Rosecrance, *The Rise of the Trading State* (New York: Basic Books, 1987); Henry Nau, *The Myth of America's Decline: Leading the World Economy into the 1990s* (New York: Oxford University Press, 1990).

5. T.J. Pempel, 'Japanese foreign economic policy', in Peter J. Katzenstein (ed.), *Between Power and Plenty, op. cit.*; Takashi Inoguchi, 'Japan's images and options: not a challenger, but a supporter', *Journal of Japanese Studies*, Vol. 12, No. 1, Winter 1986, pp.95–119, included as Chapter 1 of this volume; Takashi Inoguchi, 'Four Japanese scenarios for the future', *International Affairs*, Vol. 65, No. 1, Winter 1988-9, pp.15–28, included as Chapter 8 of this volume; Takashi Inoguchi, 'Shaping and sharing Pacific dynamism', *Annals of the American Academy of Political and Social Sciences*, No. 505, September 1989, pp.46–55, included as Chapter 6 of this volume; Takashi Inoguchi and Daniel I. Okimoto (eds), *The Political Economy of Japan*, Volume 2: *The Changing International Context* (Stanford: Stanford University Press, 1988); William Nester, *Japan's Coming to Power over East Asia and the World*, (London: Macmillan, 1989).

6. Peter Katzenstein, *Between Power and Plenty, op. cit.*; Peter Katzenstein, *Small States in World Markets: Industrial Policy in Europe* (Ithaca: Cornell University Press, 1985); Peter A. Gourevitch, *Politics at Hard Times: Comparative Responses to International Economic Crisis*, (Ithaca: Cornell University Press, 1987). Ronald Rogowski, *Commerce and Coalitions: How Trade Affects Domestic Political Alignments* (Princeton, NJ: Princeton University Press, 1990).

7. W.G. Beasley, 'The foreign threat and the opening of the ports' in Marius Jansen (ed.), *The Cambridge History of Japan*, Volume 5: *The Nineteenth Century* (Cambridge: Cambridge University 1989), pp.259–307; Akira Iriye, 'Japan's drive to great-power status', *ibid.*, pp.721–82.

8. Richard Samuels, *The Business of the Japanese State* (Ithaca: Cornell University Press, 1987); Daniel I. Okimoto, *Between MITI and the Market: Japanese Industrial Policy for High Technology* (Stanford:

Stanford University Press, 1988); David Friedman, *Misunderstood Miracle*, (Ithaca: Cornell University Press, 1986).

9. R. Rogowski, *op. cit.*

10. T. Inoguchi, 'Trade, technology and security' and 'Four Japanese scenarios for the future', *op. cit.*

11. John Zysman, *Governments, Markets, and Growth* (Ithaca: Cornell University Press, 1983); John Zysman and Stephen Cohen, *Manufacturing Matters: The Myth of the Post-Industrial Economy* (New York: Basic Books, 1987); Chalmers Johnson *et al.*, *Politics and Productivity: How Japan's Development Strategy Works* (Cambridge, Mass.: Ballinger, 1989).

12. Gary Saxonhouse, 'The micro- and macro-economics of foreign sales to Japan', in William Cline (ed.), *Trade Policy for the 1980s* (Cambridge, Mass.: MIT Press, 1988), pp. 157–93; Gary Saxonhouse, 'Comparative advantage, structural adaptation and Japanese performance', in Inoguchi and Okimoto (eds), *op. cit.*

13. Chalmers Johnson, *MITI and the Japanese Miracle* (Stanford: Stanford University Press, 1983); Yasukichi Yasuba and Kozo Yamamura (eds), *The Political Economy of Japan, Volume 1: The Domestic Transformation* (Stanford: Stanford University Press, 1987); Chalmers Johnson *et al.*, *op. cit.*

14. Chalmers Johnson, *op. cit.*; Chalmers Johnson *et al.*, *op. cit.*; Richard Samuels, *op. cit.*; Daniel I. Okimoto, 'Political inclusivity', in T. Inoguchi and D. I. Okimoto (eds), *op. cit.*, pp. 305–44.

15. Kent Calder, 'Japanese foreign economic formation: explaining the reactive state', *World Politics*, Vol. XL, No. 4, July 1988, pp. 517–41; Kent Calder, *Crisis and Compensation: Public Policy and Political Stability in Japan, 1949–1986* (Princeton, NJ: Princeton University Press, 1989).

16. Richard Samuels, *op. cit.*; David Friedman, *op. cit.*

17. Chalmers Johnson, 'Sino-Japanese relations, 1972–1985', in Herbert Ellison (ed.), *The Sino-Soviet Conflict and the Pacific Quadrille* (Boulder, Colo.: Westview Press, 1987), pp. 57–73; Tomoyuki Kojima, *Kawariyuku Chugoku no seiji shakai* (The changing political society in China) (Tokyo: Seri shobo, 1989); Gerald Segal and Akihiko Tanaka (eds), *China's Reforms in Crisis* (London: Royal Institute of International Affairs, 1990); Allen Whiting, *China Eyes Japan* (Berkeley: University of California Press, 1989).

18. Laura Newby, *Sino-Japanese Relations: China's Perspectives* (London: Royal Institute of International Affairs, 1988); T. Inoguchi, 'Four Japanese scenarios for the future', *op. cit.*; Wu Xuewen (ed.), *Shizilukou de Riben* (Japan at the crossroads) (Beijing: Shishi chupansche, 1988).

19. T. Inoguchi, 'Shaping and sharing Pacific dynamism', *op. cit.*

20. Ezra Vogel, *One Step Ahead in China: Guangdong Under Reform* (Cambridge: Mass., Harvard University Press, 1989).

21. JETRO (Japan External Trade Organization), *Chogoku: Jiang Zemin taisei iko go no seiji keizai* (China: Its Political Economy since the Transition to the Jiang Zemin Regime), (Tokyo: JETRO, 1990).
22. *ibid.*
23. T. Kojima, *op. cit.*
24. *ibid.*
25. Saburo Okita, *Japan in the World Economy of the 1980s* (Tokyo: University of Tokyo Press, 1989).
26. Takashi Inoguchi, 'Japan's images and options: not a challenger, but a supporter' *Journal of Japanese Studies*, Vol. 12, No. 1, Winter 1986, pp. 95–119; T. Inoguchi, 'Trade, technology and security', *op. cit.*; T. Inoguchi, 'Four Japanese scenarios for the future', *op. cit.*; T. Inoguchi, 'Nichi-Bei kankei no rinen to kozo' (The ideas and structures of Japan–US relations), *Leviathan: The Japanese Journal of Political Science*, No. 5, Autumn 1989, pp. 7–39, included as Chapter 2 of this volume; Inoguchi and Okimoto, *op. cit.*
27. Edward Lincoln, *Japan: Facing Economic Maturity* (Washington, DC: Brookings Institution, 1989); Edward Lincoln, *Japan's Unequal Trade* (Washington, DC: Brookings Institution, 1990).
28. T. Inoguchi, 'Four Japanese scenarios for the future', *op. cit.*
29. T. Inoguchi, 'The emergence of the predominant faction: domestic changes and their security implications', paper presented at conference on 'Beyond the Cold War in the Pacific', San Diego, California, 7–9 June 1990.
30. T. Inoguchi, 'Nichi-Bei kankei no rinen to kozo', *op. cit.*; D. I. Okimoto, 'Political inclusivity', *op. cit.*
31. K. Calder, *op. cit.*
32. T. Inoguchi, 'Trade, technology and security', *op. cit.*
33. T. Inoguchi, 'Shaping and sharing Pacific dynamism', *op. cit.*
34. T. Inoguchi, 'Japanese responses to Europe 1992: implications for the United States', paper presented to conference on Europe 1992, Washington, DC, 4–6 October 1989.
35. T. Inoguchi, *ibid.*
36. *Nihon keizai shimbun,* evening edition, 16 November 1989. The Polish State News Agency reported on the results of the opinion poll conducted in November 1989.
37. *Asahi shimbun,* morning edition, 14 July 1990.
38. On Japanese economic thought, see for instance Sugihara Shiro *et al., Nihan no Keizai shiso yonhyakunen* (Japanese Economic Thought for the Last 400 Years) (Tokyo: Nihan Keizai Hyoronsha, 1990). For discussion of many developmental models, see Manfred Bienefeld and Martin Godfrey (eds), *The Struggle for Development* (New York: Wiley, 1982).
39. Koichi Hamada, *The Political Economy of International Monetary Interdependence* (Cambridge, Mass.: MIT Press, 1985).
40. Chalmers Johnson, 'Political institutions and economic

performance. the government business relations in Japan, South Korea and Taiwan', in Frederic Deyo (ed.), *The Political Economy of the New Asian Industrialism* (Ithaca: Cornell University Press, 1986), pp. 136–64.

Part IV:
Pacific dynamism

6

Shaping and sharing Pacific dynamism

Dynamism – this is the best single word to characterize the evolution of the Pacific region over the past decade. Economic growth, trade expansion, and exchange-rate movements – the rise of most currencies in the Pacific region against the US dollar – demonstrate the profound importance of the Pacific region in shaping global adjustments of international relations and the world economy.[1]

Dynamism contains both positive and negative aspects.[2] Positively, it means vigor and aggressiveness. Negatively, it means uncertainty and unpredictability. Because Pacific dynamism brings increasing prosperity to the Pacific region and to the entire world with its vigorous growth and expansion, it is termed positive. From this side of the looking glass, forging economic interdependence with a prosperous economic region brings economic benefits. The dramatic expansion of the Japanese market and, to a lesser degree, the markets of South Korea and Taiwan promotes the absorption of manufactured goods from the rest of the world: Japan's share of manufactured goods in total imports for the period 1979–88 has increased from 26.0 per cent to slightly higher than 48.0 per cent.[3]

At the same time, the very vigor and aggressiveness of this economic activity has been helping to create uncertainty and unpredictability in the whole arena of trade and even sometimes in security arrangements. The awesome Pacific economic growth and trade expansion in manufactured goods for the last decade and, more recently, the staggering trade surplus and financial power of Japan, Taiwan, and Korea have been causing a variety of counteractions from various countries. Thus, from the other side of the looking glass, the rapid emergence of competitive economic actors has been enormously disruptive, forcing the rest of the world to counteract with other means. One strong piece of evidence is the surge of protectionism and regionalism throughout the world in the last couple of years. Other examples range from the inability of the Uruguay Round on the General Agreement on Tariffs and Trade (GATT) to come to accord for midterm review in December 1988, to the open militancy of Americans against Pacific Asians and West Europeans using their unilateral interpretations of unfair trade practices, to the ratification by the Canadians of the US–Canadian bilateral free-trade agreement in December 1988, and finally to the increased self-confidence of West Europeans in devising trade and investment rules of their own toward further European integration in 1992.

In the rest of this article, I shall first describe the three major features of Pacific Asian economic relations. Then I shall analyze how the somewhat weakened leadership of the two superpowers affects the course that Pacific dynamism will take. Third, I shall focus on the considerations and calculations of the Japanese in shaping and sharing Pacific dynamism and in adapting to the counteractions of the other major actors. I shall place the Japanese conceptions of Pacific dynamism first in a historical perspective, second in relation to longer-term scenarios of Japan's place in the world, and third in the context of current policy alternatives.

Three major features of Pacific dynamism

In focusing on intra-Pacific economic interactions, three major features emerge: the flying-goose formation of economic growth, the enhancement of horizontal interactions within the Pacific Asia region, and strains between the Pacific Asia region and other parts of the world, particularly North America and Western Europe.

The flying-goose formation

The well-known phrase 'flying-goose formation' was invented by Kaname Akamatsu to characterize the development pattern of East and Southeast Asia.[4] Like flying geese forming a triangular pattern headed by their leader, Pacific Asian development is spearheaded by Japan, which is followed by the Asian newly industrializing countries (NICs), including South Korea, Taiwan, Hong Kong, Singapore, Malaysia, and Thailand, and now is followed increasingly by some other countries of the Association of Southeast Asian Nations (ASEAN) and, to a far lesser degree, China, Vietnam, North Korea, and the Soviet Union. Dynamism diffuses from Japan to Korea, Taiwan, Hong Kong, and Singapore, and further to Malaysia, Thailand, Indonesia, the Philippines, and Brunei as well as to China, Vietnam, North Korea, and the Soviet Union. Uneven development in Pacific Asia has forced countries to focus energy on those industrial sectors nascently competitive with the rest and to gain from exports in a gradual fashion when its own market is not sufficiently large. The open and large market of the United States and the US-led free-trade regime have been indispensable to this pattern of economic development.

There are two other mechanisms in this development pattern: 1) the success of early starters in Pacific Asia has been emulated selectively to accelerate the latecomers' catch-up process; and 2) the gradually lost competitiveness of early starters in some sectors enables latecomers to rise through the former's shift of production site from home to the latter. Thus, for instance, some Japanese electronics firms used to produce goods in Taiwan and Korea when Japanese wages and other costs soared, but as Taiwanese and Korean costs steadily rose, they began to operate more in Thailand and the Philippines. UNIDEN, an electronics company based in Japan, is now in the process of shifting all its production sites from Taiwan and Hong Kong to the Philippines and China, thus diffusing economic benefits to the Philippines and China as well.[5]

Horizontal interactions enhanced

As Pacific dynamism has unfolded to the entire region, the intraregional interactions in Pacific Asia have increased dramatically. Foremost in importance among them is the increasingly horizontal relationship between Japan and the Asian NICs, as exemplified by the dramatic increase in Japan's importation of manufactured goods from Asian NICs and ASEAN countries, registering around 50 per cent per annum since 1985.[6] There has also been a drastic decrease in exports from the Asian NICs of Korea, Taiwan, and Hong Kong to the United States as a proportion of their total exports, decreasing to one-third in 1988 from the level of one-half in 1985.[7] Among the Asian NICs as well, the complex trade pattern has emerged so as to make each country a horizontal trade partner of the others; such a relationship obtains especially between Taiwan and Korea. Although the size of such trade has not become as large as that in the European Community, the direction of the movement has become unmistakably clear. Also not to be overlooked are the vigorous moves by the Asian NICs in trade with, direct investment in, and, more recently, economic aid to some ASEAN countries, China, North Korea, and Vietnam. For instance, Taiwan is now first in terms of direct investment flows in the Philippines, surpassing both Japan and the United States. These moves are positive, as they help shape the region with regional resources rather than relying too heavily on extraregional markets. They are positive also as they make the angle of the flying-goose formation less acute and more obtuse, helping to foster a sense of equality.

Strains and stresses with other major partners

Pacific Asia must cope with the increasing salience of stresses and strains in its relationship with North America and Western Europe. In terms of saving rate, growth rate, trade surplus, and financing power, Japan and the Asian NICs are clearly one of the destabilizing forces in the world economy just as the United States and debt-ridden middle-income countries are at the other extreme. Pacific Asia has thus become party to trade frictions. As the United States increasingly resorts to what is called aggressive bilateral peacekeeping in trade,[8] frustrated as it has been with the GATT's multilateralist experiences for promoting market liberalization, these stresses and strains are most likely to continue to exist. Not only the issue of trade surplus but also all sorts of other issues characterize the rapidly intertwining economic partnership between Pacific Asia on one hand and North America and Western Europe on the other. They include intellectual property, direct investment codes, service trade, agricultural subsidies, exchange-rate regulation, non-tariff barriers, industrial targeting, specific reciprocity, inward-looking regionalism, and block formation through bilateralism.

Three features are important when we look into the considerations and calculations of Japan concerning Pacific dynamism. First, the still-unfolding pattern of uneven development in Pacific Asia means that Pacific Asia continues to have enormous room for activating and intensifying regional economic activities within itself. In other words, much remains to be exploited in Pacific Asia to keep its dynamism moving forward. Second, the increasing intraregional transactions, when accompanied by the relative weakening of superpower dominance and confrontation, mean the potential divergence among Pacific Asians on how to give order to a still-fluid Pacific dynamism. In other words, given the increasing prospect for the Americans to preoccupy themselves with the less than enlightened long-term globalist viewpoint, Pacific Asians might find it somewhat more difficult to organize themselves while coping with counteractions from the rest of the world to the very Pacific dynamism it has been creating.

Japanese calculations: looking backward

To examine Japanese calculations, it is necessary first to point out that Japan lives in Pacific Asia with bilateral Japanese–US ties in economic, technological, and security arenas kept perhaps incredibly high. A defeated nation with a developing-country status, Japan since 1945 has had to rely almost entirely on the generally favorable international environment that the victory of the Allied Powers, especially the United States, brought about. The most important elements of this environment were the security umbrella and the free-trade regime. Bilateral interdependence has been further enhanced as Japan has moved up from a developing country to a country whose gross national product is more than one-half that of the United States and whose per capita income has surpassed that of the United States. Two major factors have contributed to this outcome.[9]

Japanese shyness on security matters

The first factor is that by defeat and occupation – and by instinctive habit and cunning calculation – Japan has been accustomed to being shy about security and military matters since 1945. Japan's Self-Defense Forces (SDF) have been built primarily to satisfy the needs of the United States, first as an occupying power and later as an ally. They are not primarily for the defense of Japan but more intended to enhance the US military forces confronting the communist bloc. Even now the primary task of the Japanese SDF is to assist the US armed forces in the Far East and the Pacific to meet emergencies in the Pacific and around the globe. One telling fact is that the US forces in Japan are not in a position to help the Japanese land SDF on Hokkaido. Rather, they adopt a forward strategy whereby they would attack the Soviet forces deep in Soviet territories and territorial waters, with Japanese land SDF remaining vulnerable to attacking Soviet forces. Only after such an attack could the US forces start their counterattack. The Japanese maritime SDF are not equipped to make amphibious operations on Hokkaido under heavy Soviet onslaught. Both the command structure and the force structure of the Japanese SDF clearly demonstrate that they exist as one component – indispensable to be sure – of the US international security network.

Recent military buildup

The steady Japanese military buildup over the last decade now gives Japan number-three status after the Soviet Union and the

United States in terms of military expenditure. It is clear that Japan spends enormously for defense, but much of the expenditure goes to personnel, while the bulk of non-personnel expenditure goes to the purchase of some of the most sophisticated and thus most expensive weapons from the United States. This pattern of Japanese military buildup has been reinforced by the more recent criticism from abroad that Japan is a free rider of the Western alliance and that Japan should contribute more to the collective defense by shouldering more of the security role. The Japanese government has to cope with three things at the same time: 1) strong pacifism at the grass roots; 2) the still intermittently expressed reminder from abroad of the Japanese psychological debt of the last war; and 3) criticism of being a free rider in the Western alliance. The result has been this peculiar pattern of Japanese defense buildup.

Evidence of Japanese determination to meet its own defense needs can be seen in at least two areas: the resolve to manufacture its next fighter support FSXs in collaboration with the United States, yet with much more local content than its counterpart likes to think, and by its vigorous emphasis on the forthcoming midterm defense estimate on the need for land-based equipment with highly sophisticated weapons allowing for the disabling of attacking forces before they reach Japanese land.[10] These developments exemplify some of the Japanese adjustments to a changed international environment. At the same time, it remains impossible to think of the Japanese SDF without the US component. The Japanese constitutional prohibition, the near insanity of hollowing out the alliance with the United States, and the long-distance, fast-moving nature of military technology all inhibit any solitary view of national security in any strict sense of the word.

Unprecedented Japanese–US economic interdependence

The second factor in the bilateral interdependence is that the economic interdependence with the United States is perhaps unprecedented in human history. Not only trade with and investment in each country by the other but also a huge amount of Japanese purchasing of US Treasury bonds and an inestimable amount of financial trading now take place across the Pacific. The two largest and most vigorous economies of the world have every reason to increase their economic transactions with each other. Furthermore, the not-so-strange coincidence of Japanese weakness in security and American relative weakness in economic matters has reinforced Japanese economic dependence on American economic health and wealth with an astonishing speed and magnitude. To save the US dollar from falling so rapidly, Japan has been intermittently spending an enormous amount of money through monetary intervention. To liberate themselves from protectionist measures, many Japanese firms have made direct investment in the United States – no other country has so vigorously invested in the United States. The more money Japan places in the form of US dollars for whatever reasons, the more interdependent Japan and the United States become and the more difficult it is for them to disentangle themselves from the higher risk of losing an incredible value of their dollar assets overnight, given the somewhat shaky shape of the deficit-ridden US economy.

Lax US economic management

To many Japanese the problem is that the United States does not seem to manage its economy as they would like it to do. The major points of the Japanese message are the need for a drastic reduction of various expenditures including defense, the introduction of a major tax increase, the restraint of consumption through recessionary macroeconomic management, and improvement in business management and labor relations.

Some serious Japanese have begun to think about some drastic unilateral measures to discipline the somewhat lax Americans to tighten their economic management. One such move would be raising Japanese interest rates to combat quickening global inflation, which would then set off a managed decline in the dollar and US bond and stock prices, forcing the United States to cut its deficit. A more moderate step would have the United States issue bonds denominated in foreign currencies. With, for instance, yen-denominated bonds, the US government could not reduce its financial burden of debt simply by printing additional money.[11]

Japanese calculations: looking forward

It is useful to recall what kind of calculation was made by Prime Minister Yasuhiro Nakasone during his tenure of 1982–7 when his policies of economic liberalization and alliance partnership were forcefully executed.[12] First, he correctly foresaw the beneficial aspects of American Japan-bashing with respect to market liberalization and privatization of government-regulated sectors. Not only would economic liberalization help Japan to avert criticism from the United States and others against Japan's alleged protectionism, mercantilism, and free riding, but it also would help raise Japanese competitiveness. Second, his pro-US defense efforts would help Japan to skirt criticism from the United States and others for being a free rider and also set the physical and organizational foundation on which to build stronger Japanese SDF while avoiding suspicion and criticism. As someone who had prepared 32 notebooks filled with what he would do as prime minister prior to his ascension to power, Nakasone was clear about his long-cherished nationalistic goals: more economic competitiveness and stronger SDF.

Needless to say, no fundamental reversal of power between Japan and the United States has taken place during or since Nakasone's tenure despite his success in enhancing Japan's economic and military power. But the continuing economic difficulties of the United States and the steady movement toward a US–Soviet detente, along with the rise of Pacific Asia with Japan as its core driving force, have posed Japanese leaders one question: what direction should Japan take?

Japan's scenarios for the future

This is not an easy question to answer, and it has led Japanese leaders to think about Pacific dynamism much more seriously than before. To answer the question, Japanese leaders have to solve a complex set of equations involving at least three major variables: 1) economic and technological dynamism of major countries, especially Japan and the United States; 2) prospects for the dominant military technology or the possibility of nullification of nuclear arsenals either through the US–Soviet detente or through revolutionary breakthrough similar to the Strategic Defense Initiative; and 3) the debt of history as a constraining factor.[13] These are key variables in their design of future scenarios. Very briefly, they envision four major scenarios of the future in which these variables play key roles: Pax Americana phase 2, bigemony, Pax Consortis, and Pax Nipponica. I will discuss the subject more fully in Chapter 8.

Pax Americana phase 2 is a scenario of revival of American power, if in a somewhat reduced form, helped importantly by Japan's economic power. Bigemony is the condominium of the world by the United States and Japan in both economic and security arenas. Pax Consortis envisages the loosely and flexibly aligned sets of major countries concerned in major issue areas where no one is predominant. Pax Nipponica is a world where Japan enjoys a preeminent economic position with nuclear arsenals somehow nullified. My overall scenario is that in the intermediate term of a quarter century, Pax Americana phase 2 and bigemony are feasible whereas in the longer term of half a century, Pax Consortis and Pax Nipponica may become more feasible. Economic and technological dynamism is very important in differentiating Pax Americana phase 2 and Pax Nipponica. Nullification of nuclear arsenals is crucial in making feasible both Pax Consortis and Pax Nipponica because without it the two superpowers cannot remain the formidable actors. The debt of history may be crucial in differentiating Pax Americana phase 2 and bigemony since only without it can Japan become a full-fledged global military power along with the United States.

Japanese calculations: current policy alternatives

Along with these kinds of long-term scenario, there are short-term policy-oriented calculations. More concretely, two major dimensions that discriminate the four major foreign policy orientations are: 1) favoring alliance with the United States versus opposing alliance with the United States and 2) trilateralism versus Asianism.[14] The first concerns how closely Japan should align its positions with the United States while the second concerns how much weight Japan should give to Pacific Asia. In other words, the first has to do with the distance Japan should take from the United States while the second has to do with the interest Japan should give to Western Europe, one of the three pillars of industrialized regions.

Four policy alternatives

In the space created by these two dimensions, there are four quadrants that represent major policy alternatives currently discussed in Japan: 1) the northeastern quadrant represents the thinking that emphasizes the bigemonic integration with the United States and the disinclination to institute some form of Pacific Asian community; 2) the northwestern quadrant represents the inclination to take distance from the United States in security affairs but to enhance the basic trilateral economic relations; 3) the southeastern quadrant represents the policy line of retaining and even enhancing the security ties with the United States while in economic matters Pacific Asia is given much more stress than Western Europe or sometimes even North America; and 4) the southwestern quadrant represents the thinking that belittles the Japanese–US alliance and upgrades the economic ties with Pacific Asia. The northeastern quadrant is sometimes called the begemonic scenario whereas the northwestern is often called the Gaullist scenario. The southeastern scenario is sometimes called the Pax Americana phase 2 scenario while the southwestern scenario is called the Pacific Asian scenario. If the Gaullist scenario is remolded in a cooperative and conciliatory spirit, it becomes more compatible with Pax Consortis, whereas if the Pacific Asian scenario becomes globalized, then it becomes more compatible with Pax Nipponica.

Two major policy agendas

These issues in Japanese thinking about Pacific dynamism can be grouped into two basic dimensions: 1) how to maintain and enhance the friendship with the United States without being wholly subjected to what Japanese see as the somewhat aggressive, irresponsible, or erratic policy lines of the United States both in security and in economics; and 2) how to foster the good, neighborly relationship with Pacific Asia in light of its continuous dynamism and the uncertainty associated with world economic health.

Japan is somewhat uneasy about the economic difficulties of the United States and what it sees as lax economic management; Japan is similarly uneasy about the prospect of the US–Soviet detente and its ramifications for the Japanese–US security treaty and Japan's anti-Soviet defense buildup – and the possible emergence of a quadrangular balance-of-power situation in the north Pacific. In relation to the weakened leadership of the United States, Japan is concerned about the prospect of the possiblity of Japan's further involvement in international peacekeeping operations, whether along with the United Nations peacekeeping forces or with the United States armed forces or independently. On protectionism, Japan is concerned about what it sees as the abuse of unilateralism, such as the unfair-trader charge based on clause 301 of the Trade Act, and the frequent resort to bilateralism, taking advantage of its own security hegemony over allies, as is sometimes suspected of the US proposal for a bilateral free-trade agreement. Japan is concerned also about the possibilities of inward-looking regionalism and malign protectionism in Western Europe and, to a lesser extent, in North America – and Japan is increasingly convinced of the need to enhance the regional basis on which it may be able to absorb or mitigate some negative consequences of inward-looking regionalism and malign protectionism that might get momentum in other regions of the world. On Pacific Asia, Japan is concerned about the negative feeling occasionally expressed there about Japan's debt to the region and about the constraints these feelings create for Japan's attempt to enhance what it terms regional cooperation in Pacific Asia.

The basic problem confronting Japan is the paradox of dynamism. Namely, the very dynamism that Japan and Pacific Asia now demonstrate helps to create the kind of uncertainty and unpredictability of the world economy and international relations that may undermine the very foundation of the prosperity that Japan and Pacific Asia now enjoy. Pacific dynamism invites counteractions from major actors: US bilateralism, Europe's regionalism, and the superpowers' detente, all intended either to enable self-restructuring and acquire competitiveness or to bring in self-closure and rest in benign protectionism – or both. To see the outcome of these complex Pacific interactions now unfolding, one needs to wait.

This chapter has had the modest purpose of explicating Japanese calculations concerning Pacific dynamism.

Notes

1. Colin I. Bradford and William H. Branson, (eds.), *Trade and Structural Change in Pacific Asia* (Chicago: University of Chicago Press, 1987); Peter Drysdale, *International Economic Pluralism: Economic Policy in East Asia and the Pacific* (New York: Columbia University Press, 1988).

2. Takashi Inoguchi, 'The international political economy of the Pacific dynamism', in *Japan's Growing External Assets: A Medium for Regional Growth?* ed. Susumu Awanohara (Hong Kong: Linnan College, Centre for Asian Pacific Studies, 1989, pp. 617–77.

3. Peter Drysdale and Ross Garnaut, 'A Pacific free trade area?', paper delivered at 'More Free Trade Areas? Outlook for World Trade Policy'. Conference of the Institute for International Economics, Washington, DC, 31 Oct.–1 Nov. 1988.

4. Akamatsu Kaname, *Sekai keizairon* (World Economics) (Tokyo: Kunimoto shobo, 1965).

5. *Nihon keizai shimbun*, 23 May 1988.

6. Drysdale and Garnaut, 'Pacific free trade area?', *op. cit.*

7. *Nihon keizai shimbun,* 22 November 1988.

8. Robert Baldwin and J. David Richardson, 'Recent U.S. trade policy and its global implications', in *Trade and Structural Change*, ed. Bradford and Branson, pp. 121–55. See also Paula Stern and Paul A. London, 'A reaffirmation of US trade policy', *Washington Quarterly*, 11(4):55–71 (Autumn 1988); Stephen Krasner, 'Trade conflicts and the common defense', *Political Science Quarterly*, 101(5):787–806 (1986).

9. Takashi Inoguchi, 'The ideas and structures of foreign policy: looking ahead with caution', in *The Political Economy of Japan, Volume 2, The Changing International Context*, ed. Takashi Inoguchi and Daniel I. Okimoto (Stanford: Stanford University Press, 1988), pp. 23–63, 490–500.

10. For FSXs, see *Asahi shimbun*, 4 June 1988; *Nihon keizai shimbun*, 26 December 1988. See also Takashi Inoguchi, 'Trade, technology and security: implications for East Asia and the West', *Adelphi Papers*, 218:39–55 (1987), included as Chapter 4 of this volume.

For the midterm task estimate, see *Yomiuri shimbun*, 11 May 1988; Japan Defense Agency, *White Paper on Defense 1988* (Tokyo: Government Printing Office, 1988).

11. *International Herald Tribune*, 23 December 1988.
12. Takashi Inoguchi, 'The legacy of a weathercock prime minister', *Japan Quarterly*, 34(4):367–70 (Oct.-Dec. 1987), included as Chapter 4 of this volume.
13. Takashi Inoguchi, 'Four Japanese scenarios for the future', *International Affairs*, 65(1) (Winter 1988–9), included as Chapter 8 of this volume.
14. Takashi Inoguchi, 'Japan's images and options: not a challenger, but a supporter', *Journal of Japanese Studies*, 12(1):95–119 (Winter 1986), included as Chapter 1 of this volume; *idem*, 'Ideas and structures of foreign policy'.

7

Sino-Japanese relations: problems and prospects

The year 1989

If the late Zhou Enlai was correct in claiming that it is still too early to assess the significance of the French Revolution of 1789, it is much too early to assess the significance of the year 1989.[1] Yet, in 1989 so many seemingly important events took place that the year is likely to be regarded as the turning point of the period since 1945. These events included the deepening of US–Soviet detente, the breakup of the Soviet empire, the breakdown of barriers between East and West Germany, growing West European integration, and the disengagement of the United States and the Soviet Union from confrontation in the Third World. The Tiananmen Square incident and its impact on Sino-Japanese relations must also be included in any assessment of 1989.

Although it is too early to evaluate fully the impact of the Tiananmen Square incident on the Chinese development and on Sino-Japanese relations, it does not seem too impetuous to claim that 1989 stands as a clear watershed in the evolution of Sino-Japanese relations since normalization of diplomatic relations in 1972. At the same time, it is also undeniable that current Sino-Japanese relations are full of uncertainties, as both domestic and international forces shaping their bilateral relations are best characterized as fluid. With these caveats in mind, I will nevertheless attempt to characterize Sino-Japanese relations and to speculate on their future course.

Problems

Three sets of problems have surfaced throughout the evolution of Sino-Japanese relations in the post-war period: 1) the debt of history, 2) economic interdependence, and 3) the strategic configuration of power in the region. In this section I will briefly summarize the basic nature of these problems.

The debt of history

Casting its shadow over the entire spectrum of Sino-Japanese relations, the debt of history refers to the negative record of Japanese actions toward the Chinese and other Asian peoples during the 1930s and 1940s. A problem arises because both countries entertain very different notions about the debt of history.[2] The Chinese regard it as a cardinal starting point in their bilateral relationship with Japan, whereas the Japanese tend to view it somewhat ambivalently. This Japanese ambivalence stems in large part from the conception of their historical identity. The Japanese have tended to regard the history of the 1930s and 1940s in a mix of the West German, Austrian, and East German images of the Second World War. The West German image emphasizes German guilt. In contrast, the Austrian image sees the Austrians as being victims and thus not guilty, while the East German image emphasizes the role of communist leaders as resisters against fascism.[3] Naturally, even among the Japanese, the first image carries some weight, especially when they recall the atrocities and suffering other Asians went through because of Japanese imperial expansion. However, the second image tends to enter the Japanese mind when viewing their war against the United States and other Western powers as imperial expansion justified by the necessity of avoiding being 'swallowed up' by a Western power. The second image tends to the atomic bombing of Hiroshima and Nagasaki are recalled. The third image, although it hardly applies, was called to mind when, for instance, the Japanese masses opposed the UN Peace Cooperation bill, which would have allowed the Self-Defense Forces' support of the US-led multilateral forces against Iraq.

The guilt of exercising mililtary force to defend Japan's self-interest was expressed.

More directly, many Japanese want to believe that their historical efforts since the mid-nineteenth century have been legitimate despite their negative ramifications. With Japan's growing economic power, intensifying international criticism, and increasing national self-confidence, the debt of history appears to have been watered down, hence the trouble with history textbooks and concern over a revival of militarism.[4]

On the Chinese side, the debt of history provides very convenient leverage in many situations. First, by suggesting to the Japanese their enormous indebtedness to China, China can solicit Japan's assistance in its modernization efforts. Second, the Chinese regime can use Japan as a scapegoat in order to divert attention from its own shortcomings in the eyes of its people. Third, the Chinese masses can forget their own shortcomings by blaming foreigners.[5]

Economic interdependence

The Chinese and Japanese economies seem to be complementary in two ways that encourage economic interdependence between the two countries. First, for China a close economic relationship with Japan is necessary to modernize its economy, while for Japan the potential of the China market is irresistible in the long run. Second, China is a producer and exporter of the energy and natural resources Japan lacks, while Japan produces and exports many consumer and capital goods China needs. These two economic complementarities have been linked by China to the debt of history and China takes advantage of this factor to promote its modernization efforts. Since China did not seek war reparations from Japan when the countries normalized relations, nor at the conclusion of the Peace and Friendship Treaty, Chinese leaders expect Japan to assist fully in their nation's modernization efforts.[6]

After the Peace and Friendship Treaty was concluded and China commenced its economic reforms in 1978, it was natural that an economic interdependence should be gradually forged between the two countries. Yet, economic interdependence is never easy to manage; economic interactions between these very divergent economic systems have been plagued with severe difficulties.[7] The Chinese state has had enormous problems reforming and managing its socialist command economy because it is ill-equipped to handle market forces and because businesses are prone to use the mixed-socialist system for dubious profiteering. The business cycle of the command economy – from the launching of a five-year economic plan, through investment booms and an overheating of the economy to drastic economic contraction – has also strained economic interdependence. The small size of the Chinese economy, considerable constraints on capitalist economic activities, and uncertainty over the success of China's reform efforts have all tended to discourage Japanese business from more vigorous economic participation.

As a result, during boom years the Japanese export of capital and consumer goods has predictably produced enormous Chinese trade deficits *vis-à-vis* Japan. This in turn causes China to be very critical of its trading partner. During periods of recession, restraints on the import of Japanese goods as well as tight economic management have tended to generate social and political unrest, which are potential sources for anti-regime and anti-foreign social and political movements. Aside from this pattern of economic problems arising from the cyclical nature of the reforming command economy, a general gap in expectations has tended to generate disappointment on both sides. For instance, often when the Chinese reflect on how Japanese direct investment in China constitutes only 1 per cent of all Japanese direct investment abroad, they lament that the Japanese are oblivious to Chinese generosity and wonder how the Japanese can underestimate the potential of the China market.[8]

Strategic power configuration in the region

The strategic configuration of power in the region refers to the relative standing and weight of China and Japan within the Asian Pacific region. This region includes the United States, the Soviet Union, Taiwan, the two Koreas, Vietnam, and the

ASEAN countries. This factor has shaped the evolution of Sino-Japanese relations. In particular, China's and Japan's respective relations with the United States and the Soviet Union and their relative power *vis-à-vis* each other have been important.

Relations with the United States and Soviet Union were especially important in the 1970s. The normalization of Sino-Japanese relations in 1972 was in large part due to the Sino-American rapprochement the previous year, while the conclusion of the Peace and Friendship Treaty in 1978 was accomplished in an atmosphere of growing Chinese perceptions of a 'hegemonic' military threat from the Soviet Union, which concluded an alliance with Vietnam in 1978. Needless to say, the United States and the Soviet Union remain important game players in Pacific Asia. Yet, as far as Sino-Japanese relations are concerned, the direct impact of the two superpowers has been diminishing since the early 1980s.

The relative powers of China and Japan have become more important as the relative weight and overall standing of the two countries in the Asian Pacific region have shifted in Japan's favor. This is a result of the disparity in their economic development and the steadily weakening interest in China by the United States and the Soviet Union and is evident in comparing the relative stature of China and Japan in 1972 and 1990. In 1972 China was a major political power conducting a game of great power diplomacy *vis-à-vis* the United States and the Soviet Union, while Japan was little more than an emerging economic giant. At that time, both countries complemented each other, each with relative strengths in different domains. In 1990, not only was China unable to move forward on the path of vigorous economic development, thus being left far behind Japan, but it had also lost much interest in playing a great power game during a period in which the United States and the Soviet Union each reduced their respective interest in China for differing reasons. In contrast, Japan has become potentially a major player in the power game. Yet despite all the swollen expectations held by the United States (for Japan to assume greater international responsibility) and by the USSR (for Japan to assist in its transition to a market economy), Japan has been incapacitated by domestic difficulties. In sum, China and Japan have been placed in very different situations.

As a result of these changes, Sino-Japanese relations seem to mirror the kind of reversal associated with the bilateral balance of power. In the 1970s and 1980s, China, a deft game-player of diplomacy, was widely seen as setting the pace and tone of Sino-Japanese relations. Since the 1980s, Japan has become a 'silent power', quietly setting the pace of relations based on its economic power.[9]

The current state of Sino-Japanese relations

Having made these admittedly oversimplified characterizations, I will now attempt to assess the current state of Sino-Japanese relations. It seems that the crux of the matter is how to resolve the locus of three major problems: the debt of history, economic interdependence, and the strategic power configuration. The rapid changes within the international system since 1989 have had important consequences for Sino-Japanese relations.

The deepening of US–Soviet detente and the erosion of the East–West confrontation have made the issue of the debt of history much more salient as a united Germany and Japan inevitably play more prominent roles in world affairs. The possibility of an economically powerful Germany and Japan again reasserting themselves in isolation from others is a concern of some nations. Apprehension has been aroused in some quarters by, for example, German reunification, German domination of a European economic and monetary union, German–Soviet entente, Chancellor Kohl's statement of his intention to seek revision of the constitution, triggered by the Gulf crisis, and the Bundesbank's hike in interest rates to 6.5 per cent to the displeasure of the United States with its interest rate of 6.0 per cent. Japan's initial reluctance and decision later to dispatch its Self-Defense Forces top rescue refugees in the Gulf crisis (the first overseas effort in the SDF's history), the Bank of Japan's move to coordinate monetary policy in Pacific Asia, and Japanese agitation about foreign labor have aroused apprehension for different reasons in some quarters as well.[10]

After partially cleaning up its post-Tiananmen Square difficulties, China's attention has turned to concerns about Japan's response to the Gulf crisis. It has not been Japan's reluctance to play a more visible role in the crisis, but the decision to send Self-Defense Forces to the Middle East that has triggered the largely negative reaction by China. Before the Gulf crisis, China had somewhat moderated its approach to the debt of history issue after the Tiananmen Square incident isolated it from virtually all major foreign financial players abroad. In June 1989, the ratio of foreign loans, approximately two-thirds of which are Japanese, to central government revenues was as high as five to seven. After major foreign monetary flows dried up following the Tiananmen Square incident, the Chinese central government therefore faced a severe economic crisis. This problem was further exacerbated by the government's reform policy of decentralization, which resulted in sluggish growth in central government tax revenues and a large increase in local government tax revenues in areas of rapid economic growth. Japan's hesitancy to criticize China's suppression of human rights because of the debt of history is evident.

In conjunction with the 1990 Western economic summit communiqué, which noted Japan's decision to resume its loans to China, China and Japan started vigorously to increase their interaction. Both nations felt isolated in the latter half of 1989 and the first half of 1990. The Tiananmen Square incident isolated China, and US–Soviet detente reduced the importance of China in the superpowers' cognitive maps. The Recruit scandal, in which the Recruit Cosmos company bribed major figures in political parties, bureaucracy and journalism and forced Prime Minister Noboru Takeshita to resign from office in 1990, paralyzed the Japanese government with the inevitable consequence of diplomatic inaction in the face of world pressure for Japan to adapt itself to the changing international environment. As US–Soviet relations warmed, a series of acute crises cooled Japan–US relations and left Japan isolated, at a time when it was especially eager to move toward rapprochement with the Soviet Union. Hence, there were several compelling reasons for China and Japan to attempt to collaborate despite their respective domestic problems. Yet for China, preoccupied with its domestic economy and politics, the legacy of past relations with Japan has always encouraged it to pull back from a close collaboration. This has been reinforced by other Asian nations' intensifying criticism of Japan, whether over the shadow of history, South Korean criticism of Japan's attempted rapprochement with North Korea, or Taiwan's resentment of Japan's handling of the Senkaku Islands dispute.[11]

The forging of economic interdependence between China and Japan has been carefully managed by both countries. The Chinese government tightened controls over government expenditures, money supply, and imports after the Tiananmen Square incident, while the Japanese government froze its financial loans to China and Japanese businesses scaled down their activities in China. As a result, a reversal of the trade balance has taken place, with China now registering a trade surplus with Japan. Yet, despite all these setbacks, the basic structure of Sino-Japanese economic interdependence has been gradually enhanced as China has been steadily incorporated into the capitalist Asian Pacific economic orbit.[12] This is especially true because the United States has reduced its interest in China for strategic and human rights reasons and because Western Europe is preoccupied with its economic union in 1992 and expanding economic ties with former socialist countries in Eastern Europe. The development is especially salient to China's coastal provinces, encompassing 200 million people. In tandem with the gradual loosening of tight economic policy at the center and with the retention and revival of Zhaoist reform policy, with emphasis placed by Secretary General Zhao Ziyang on initiatives and responsibilities in business whether it is agriculture, manufacturing, distribution or foreign trade, the kinds of issues that have intermittently been conspicuous between China and Japan may flare up again. These include trade deficits, Japan's reluctance to transfer technology, fewer concessionary loans, the flooding of the Chinese market with Japanese products, difficulties in supplying energy and machinery parts, and difficulties in transportation and distribution.[13]

The strategic configuration of power is becoming extremely fluid in the Asian Pacific region with the slow yet steady dissolution of the Cold War framework. China's foreign policy made good use of the Gulf crisis and the Beijing Asian Games to recover from its post-Tiananmen isolation. The Gulf crisis gave China an opportunity to join the mainstream of the emerging post-Cold War framework by participating in the economic sanctions against Iraq and to elevate its reputation by rescuing Chinese of all nationalities, whether from China, Taiwan, or Hong Kong, in Iraq and Kuwait. The Asian Games were a success in that they enabled China to demonstrate to the rest of the world that order and calm had been restored.

China has thus far adapted well to the post-Cold War period. It has restored diplomatic relations with Indonesia and has also been strengthening its economic and political ties with South Korea, mending fences with Vietnam, and trying to bring peace to Cambodia. Its relationship with the Soviet Union is peaceful and friendly largely because both countries are preoccupied with domestic difficulties. Its relationship with the United States may start to move in a better direction with the extension of most favored nation status to China. Although Congress may have criticized China's record on human rights, it did not nullify President Bush's extension of most favored nation status to China. China's relationship with Japan has also been moving in a better direction. Japan's unfreezing of economic aid to China is one factor, while China's restoration of political order and reactivation of its economy are another.

Both China and Japan seem to be moving toward military consolidation.[14] China increased its military budget very substantially in 1990 for the first time since it began undertaking reforms in 1978. It seems to be attempting to transform its coastal navy into a force that can project its power in the region. Although Japan has been cutting the rate of increase in its military spending, it has been attempting to enhance its overall military capabilities. The fluidity of the post-Cold War period seems to encourage both countries to strengthen their militaries in order to meet possible local challenges and problems that have been heretofore largely suppressed by the Cold War framework.

A big question mark to both countries is the United States. Even if the United States remains the only country able to project its military power on a global scale, it is not entirely clear how long the United States can continue to sustain its Gulf-crisis type of commitments given current financial constraints. Furthermore, it is not clear whether the Japan–US security arrangement will continue without fairly drastic changes. On the other hand, the global trend toward further detente seems to be steadily permeating Pacific Asia as well, which obviously encourages Japan and China to seek arms-reduction and confidence-building measures in the region. Yet, uncertainty prevails as to how tension reduction can be multilaterally or bilaterally accomplished in Pacific Asia. Thus, both kinds of uncertainty seem to be leading the two countries in the direction of a cautious but steady enhancement of their military capabilities. This observation seems to apply to virtually all the Asian Pacific countries, except the United States and the Soviet Union. How this tendency will collide with the global detente and its gradual permeation of the Asian Pacific region is difficult to say and creates uncertainty and fluidity within the region.[15]

China's apprehension about Japan's possible reemergence as a military power seems to be increasing at a time when the Japanese government, in an effort to respond to calls for assuming greater international responsibilities, has tried to legislate its UN Peace Cooperation bill, whereby the Self-Defense Forces could be dispatched abroad. Japanese obliviousness to the legacy of past relations with China, which the Chinese always try to impress on Japan, combined with Japan's possible reemergence as a military power, naturally arouses an instinctive negative reaction from China. Yet, the Chinese are aware that there is no immediate and direct means of effectively changing Japan's policy alone and that China desperately needs Japan's assistance for economic development.

Japan seems to hold a different set of apprehensions about China. It is concerned about the consequences of possible anarchy, disorder, and even China's dissolution. A weak China is a concern for Japan, as it would destabilize the entire region. Japan's policy toward Chinese economic development and political reform seems to be based on the premise of preventing China from declining into a very weak and disintegrating nation, rather than on the premise of preventing it from becoming a strong and menacing nation.[16]

Conclusion

Both China and Japan appear to be mindful of and determined to control what should be the basic assumption in managing their relations: the fact that a breakdown in relations would have immense negative consequences for both countries and for the entire Asian Pacific region. Whether the debt of history, economic interdependence, and the strategic power configuration can continue to be managed depends in part on the importance attached to the relationship by the governments and peoples of both countries.

Notes

1. Simon Scharma, *Citizens: A Chronicle of the French Revolution* (New York: Vintage Books, 1989), p. xiii.
2. Laura Newby, *Sino-Japanese Relations: China's Perspective* (London: Routledge, 1988); Nakajima Mineo, *Chugoku ni jubaku sareru Nihon* (Japan that is Spellbound by China) (Tokyo: Bungei Shunju, 1987); Barry Buzan, 'Japan's future: old history versus new roles', *International Affairs*, Vol. 64, No. 4 (Autumn 1988), pp. 557–73.
3. Cf. Charles Maier, *The Unmasterable Past: History, Holocaust, and German National Identity* (Cambridge, Mass.: Harvard University Press, 1988).
4. See Newby, *op. cit.*; Kojima Tomoyuki, *Chugoku no seiji shakai* (The Political Society of China) (Tokyo: Seri Shobo, 1986), *Kawariyuku Chugoku no seiji shakai* (The Changing Political Society of China) (Tokyo: Seri Shobo, 1988), and *Kiro ni tatsu Chugoku* (China at the Crossroads) (Tokyo: Seri Shobo, 1990); Tanaka Akihiko, 'Nitchu seiji kankei' (Japanese–Chinese relations), in Okabe Tatsumi (ed.), *Chugoku o meguru kokusai kankei* (The International Relations of China) (Tokyo: Iwanami Shoten, 1990), pp. 39–76.
5. *ibid.*
6. *ibid.*
7. Minami Ryoshin, *Gendai Chugoku keizai* (The Contemporary Chinese Economy) (Tokyo: Nihon Hyronsha, 1990); Maruyama Nobuo, 'Nitchu keizai kankei' (Japanese–Chinese economic re-lations), in Okabe, *op. cit.*, pp. 77–114.
8. For further description of the generally ill-informed perception of the Chinese, see Allen Whiting, *China Eyes Japan* (Berkeley: University of California Press, 1988).
9. See Kuriyama Takakazu, 'Gekido no jidai to Nihon gaiko no shin tenkai' (The era of rapid changes and a new development in Japanese diplomacy), *Gaiko Forum* (May 1990), pp. 12–21.
10. James Kurth, 'East Asia plus mitteleuropa', Miles Kahler, ed., *The End of the Cold War in the Pacific*, University of California, Institute on Global Conflict and Cooperation, 1991, pp. 143–53.
11. This pattern was also observed in the past.

12. Takashi Inoguchi, 'Shaping and sharing Pacific dynamism', *Annals of the American Academy of Political and Social Science*, Vol. 505 (September 1989), pp. 46–55.
13. Japan External Trade Organization (JETRO), *Chugoku keizai* (The Chinese Economy) (monthly magazine), various issues.
14. Gerald Segal, 'China: encouraging signals, but worries persist', *International Herald Tribune*, 26 September 1990.
15. Takashi Inoguchi, 'Pacific Asia in the post-Cold War era', paper presented at the Yomiuri symposium on the future of socialism, 11–12 October 1990.
16. Okabe Tatsumi, 'Kongo no Chugoku to Nihon no seisaku' (China and Japan's policy from now on), International Institute for Global Peace Special Report, October 1990.

Part V:
Prospects

8

Four Japanese scenarios for the future

Japan is in an era of transition. Behind a façade of confidence in their country's future, many Japanese feel adrift in the world of the late twentieth century.[1] The Japanese energy that is currently directed overseas is no longer based, as it was in the 1960s, on a nationally orchestrated strategy. Governments are no longer sure how to guide society, or with what goals. And Japanese society itself displays its loss of faith in the belief-system so dominant in the 1960s. Today the almost blind belief of that period in the loyalty to big business firms has lost its appeal. It is not an exaggeration to say that in the 1980s Japan has been improvising its responses to the unfamiliar challenges from within and without on an *ad hoc* basis, tenaciously adhering to time-honored ways of doing things.

Bereft of a sense of direction, and uncertain about the future, Japan has been haunted by a vague angst about its future which has led it sometimes to hedge, and at least to limit, its commitment to the demands, requests, and suggestions coming from overseas that Japan, now a global economic power, should take on more global responsibility.[2] As one observer aptly put it,

Japan, in fact, does not seem to be pursuing any reasoned search for a secure place in an uncertain world, much less a plan to dominate it, but rather an energetic, opportunistic drift reminiscent of the early 1930s, with freebooting individuals and companies out giving their country a bad name while native people back home believe, like the king of Spain, that hoarding gold will make them rich. Japan has had far too many eggs – defense, trade and technology – in one US basket, considering how uncertain the US seems to be about what to do next . . .[3]

One of the salient themes which has emerged in the directionless Japanese society of the 1980s is an emphasis on traditional values: values such as perseverance, frugality, diligence, effort, family, community, sacrifice, humility, the spirit of harmony, and deference for the elderly. This fact is instructive. The problem is that these traditional values cannot be the basis for Japanese principles in guiding Japanese global policy. Prime Minister Noboru Takeshita's favourite saying, 'When you do something, sweat by yourself and give credit to others', may be the epitome of humility, generosity and altruism, but it cannot be the sole organizing principle of Japanese diplomacy. The same can be said about economic efficiency and profitability. They cannot dominate other considerations when the dollar's volatility could shake down the world economy or when the United States makes it imperative for its allies to implement tighter measures on technological transfer to some communist and Third World countries.

Apart from these traditional values and economic criteria, which are too vague to allow one to fathom how the Japanese would like to see the world evolve, what are Japan's conceptions of its global position and its global roles? In other words, how is the country shaping its scenarios of the future worlds in which Japan will occupy a not unimportant position? This article addresses these and related questions, especially in relation to burden-sharing and power-sharing with the United States in the management of the world economy and international relations.

I will present below four Japanese scenarios of the world system in 25–50 years' time, making a clear distinction between the economic and the political and security arrangements envisaged in each scenario. In each scenario, Japan's role and the degree of burden-sharing/power-sharing with the United States will also be indicated. Next, the feasibility of the four scenarios will be discussed in terms of three major conditions, assessing the relative feasibility and desirability of each scenario. The United States and Japan will be the primary focus, though other major actors, no less important to Japan than the United States, will be touched on as much as possible. Lastly, I will reflect on my findings in the light of the dominant aspirations and apprehensions of the Japanese.

But before these four scenarios are introduced, more

straightforward, if somewhat prosaic, opinion poll results will be presented. To know what opinion polls reveal is important since the scenarios of the future that follow are inevitably those conjured up largely by educated elites and not necessarily represent the prevailing moods and sentiments of ordinary Japanese people.

Japan's external role: opinion poll results

A recent opinion poll provides useful data on how the Japanese people see Japan's external role. The Public Relations Department of the Prime Minister's Office commissions annual polls on Japanese diplomacy. The most recent one, conducted in October 1987,[4] contains one question relevant to our interest. 'What kind of roles do you think Japan should play in the community of nations? Choose up to two from the list below.' The list had five items:

1. Japan should make contributions in the area of international political affairs such as the improvement of East–West relations and the mediation of regional conflicts.
2. Japan should consolidate its defence capability as a member of the Western camp.
3. Japan should contribute to the healthy development of the world economy.
4. Japan should cooperate in the economic development of developing countries.
5. Japan should make contributions in scientific, technological and cultural exchanges.

Not surprisingly, the respondents overwhelmingly preferred roles outside the security and political realms. Item (3) registered 50.4 per cent, item (4) 34.0 per cent, and item (5) 31.0 per cent, the three together adding up to 115.4 out of a total of 162.0 per cent. By contrast item (1) recorded 24.2 per cent, while item (2) registered only 7.8 per cent.

It is very clear from these figures that the Japanese are disinclined to accept a major political or security role in the world.

Another recent poll conducted by an academic team permits

us to compare the priorities attached by respondents to the
domestic and international roles the government should play.[5]
It allowed for multiple choices from among a list of priorities:

1. preventing crime and securing people's safety (law and
   order);
2. promoting technological innovation and raising productivity
   and production efficiency of the economy as a whole (economic power);
3. increasing defense capability and consolidating national
   security;
4. building roads, schools and hospitals and making life com-
   fortable (standard of living);
5. enhancing patriotism and strengthening the solidarity of the
   nation (national solidarity);
6. promoting adjustment with foreign countries in economic
   fields and improving the world economy as a whole (global
   economic welfare);
7. increasing taxes for those who can afford it and taking care
   of the poor and needy (social welfare), and
8. managing the economy to prevent inflation and unemploy-
   ment (domestic economic management).

Instead of asking, 'To which task do you want to see the government attach its first priority?', the poll stated: 'There are many
kinds of government policies nowadays. What do you think
about the emphasis which government puts on each of them?
Choose one of the following answers:

1. much more emphasis;
2. a little more emphasis;
3. keep as it is;
4. a little less emphasis;
5. no emphasis;
6. don't know;
7. no answer.'

To make comparison simple, we will look only at responses for
(1) – much more emphasis – and the following order of priorities
emerges:

1. domestic economic management (55.7 per cent);
2. law and order (55.7 per cent);
3. social welfare (45.2 per cent);
4. standard of living (44.5 per cent);
5. economic power (29.7 per cent);
6. global economic welfare (27.8 per cent);
7. national solidarity (18.8 per cent);
8. national security (11.3 per cent).

In order to make comparison across different polls possible, I must make an admittedly crude assumption. If global economic welfare is said to correspond roughly to Japan's contribution in the economic field, and national security is said to correspond roughly to Japan's contribution in the security field, then two things are immediately clear: first, the overwhelming primacy of domestic priorities, and secondly, the overwhelming weight given to economic contributions compared to security contributions to Japan's desired role in the world. All this is not surprising. However, it is very important to keep in mind that, given the preoccupation with internal affairs and the avoidance of a commitment to security matters, public acceptance of the kind of world role for Japan that is envisaged by the Japanese government and expected by foreign countries can come only slowly.

It is true that overall public acceptance of Japan's greater role in the world, whether it is of an economic nature or otherwise, has been steadily increasing for the last few years, especially during the tenure of the Nakasone Cabinet (1982–7). But this has been largely a grudging acceptance, coming only after the government has made a series of carefully calculated incremental moves without arousing too much opposition.[6] We can recall the recent breakthrough in 1987 when the defense budget exceeded the 1 per cent limit on defence expenditure over GNP,[7] and also various measures enabling enhanced security cooperation with the United States, including the Japanese decision to allow participation in the US Strategic Defense Initiative (SDI) program. But what is seen by the Japanese government as the barrier of public acceptance is still very much in evidence when it comes to Japan's security role in the world.

One recent event reinforces the impression gained from

these polls. When the United States and many other NATO countries were sending naval boats to the Persian Gulf in 1987 under the US flag, the suggestion to send the Maritime Safety Agency's boats, put forward by the prime minister and the Foreign Ministry, was defeated in Cabinet discussion because of opposition from the Ministry of Transport (which has the Maritime Safety Agency under its jurisdiction). The Cabinet secretary played a crucial role in siding with the minister of transport and with public opinion.[8] It is only against such a background that we can accurately assess Japan's conceptions of global roles, to which I now turn.

The four scenarios

The following four scenarios of the world in the next 25–50 years are seen by the Japanese as 'visions of the future'.[9] Although in some respects they overlap, they represent differing views on the future of global development, the distribution of economic and military power, and institutions for peace and development. It should also be mentioned that these scenarios have not been sketched out by the Japanese alone; both Japanese and non-Japanese have articulated their preferences, given a future in which Japan will play an enhanced role.

1. Pax Americana, phase II

This image of the future was first articulated by the Americans. It is the image of an America retaining its leading position in the world and making full use of its advantage in having created the institutions of post-Second World War order and security. This scenario depicts an America experienced in forging the 'balanced' or globalist view of the Western alliance and deftly prodding and cajoling its allies into enlightened joint action. The outline of this scenario was first made during the latter half of the 1970s, when the post-Vietnam trauma was still strong and when Soviet global influence was somewhat exaggeratedly felt in the United States. In the parlance of American political scientists, the key word was 'regimes' – rules and practices in international interest adjustment – whereby the United States would retain its enlightened hegemony and control the direction of world development. Such phrases as 'after hegemony' and 'cooperation under anarchy' – both used as book titles – epitomize the primary thrust of policy and academic interest in articulating this model of the future.[10]

This image has been intermittently put forward in different forms. Confident in the retention of America's cultural hegemony in the Gramscian sense, Bruce Russett, a Yale political scientist, criticized the declaration of America's decline and imminent demise by likening it to prematurely reporting the death of Mark Twain. More directly and bluntly, Susan Strange of the London School of Economics has asserted that US hegemony has not yet gone; the lament on 'after hegemony' is the favorite habit of American self-indulgence, she says: More recently Paul Kennedy of Yale has described the rivival of American composure and confidence, combined with the sombre recognition of the inevitability of national decline in the longer term.[11]

In Japan, this image of America's future has been a consistent favorite. Naohiro Amaya, a former vice-minister in the Ministry of International Trade and Industry, was fond of talking about 'Go-Bei' ('later United States'), as if the United States prior to Vietnam was called 'Zen-Bei' ('earlier United States'). this is an analogy with the later Han dynasty of ancient China, which was restored after 17 years of disappearance and survived for another two centuries. Similarly, Yasusuke Murakami, a well-known economist, has argued that the hegemonic cycle that has been observed for the last few centuries has ceased to repeat itself largely because the world economy has been transformed from something based on individual national economies to a much more integrated structure. His scenario delineates an America which is an enlightened and experienced *primus inter pares* in an increasingly multipolar world.[12]

This image has been a favorite one, not least because it encourages the basic retention of Japan's traditional concentration on an economic role with no drastic increase in its security role, which is largely delegated to the United States. Although Japan's profile in the world has changed a great deal in the 1980s, the Japanese preference for limiting the country's commitment to military matters, many of which are generally deemed to have dubious utility, has not been altered.

Japan's roles in Pax Americana phase II are not significantly different from its present ones. Essentially, these are primarily of an economic nature, with the bulk of global security shouldered by the United States. Even if Japan–US security cooperation is accelerated, this basic division of labour is unlikely to change. Even if Japan were to enhance its out-of-area security co-operation by sending warships to the Persian Gulf to shoulder the costs of oil imports, it would be bolstering the US-dominated world rather than becoming a main security-provider in the region. Even if Japan were to increase its security-related assistance to some Third World countries like Pakistan, Turkey, Papua New Guinea, and Honduras, the security leadership of the United States would remain strong. Needless to say, there are those who argue that Japan will start in due course to exert influence by accumulating credit in the United States and other countries. But in this scenario Japanese self-assertiveness will be restrained by various domestic and international factors.

Japan's regional roles in this scenario will be heavily economic. More concretely, Japan will become the vital core of the Pacific growth crescent, encompassing three areas: 1) northern Mexico, the Pacific United States and Canada, 2) Japan, and 3) the Pacific – the Asian newly industrializing countries, coastal China, the Association of SouthEast Asian (ASEAN) countries and Oceania.[13] The incorporation of the second and the third economic groups into the extended US economic zone will be a vital factor in a US revival. In short, Japan's role in this scenario will be to link the US economy with the Asian Pacific economies in a more balanced manner than today. In this scenario, the current US efforts to liberalize the Pacific Asian markets, revalue local currency–dollar exchange rates and promote burden-sharing in development aid and finance and international security will be given further momentum. At the same time, Pacific Asian nationalistic anti-Americanism will be considerably restrained. Perhaps it is important to note that Pax Americana phase II will need a no less vigorous Western Europe. An enlarged and enhanced European Community (EC) will remain a pillar of this scenario. But if it degenerates into regional protectionism of the sort that can be glimpsed in the tougher EC anti-dumping policy on printing machines, through arrogance derived from an expected enlarged size and power, then it will elicit a negative reaction from the United States and Japan.

2. 'Bigemony'

This second scenario for the future has been propagated by economists and businessmen, fascinated by the rapid development and integration of what Robert Gilpin, a Princeton political scientist, calls the 'nichibei [Japan–US] economy'. That is to say, the economies of Japan and the United States have become one integrated economy of a sort. C. Fred Bergsten, an economist who worked as a senior bureaucrat under the Carter Administration and is now director of the Institute for International Economics, coined the word 'bigemony', which denotes the primordial importance of the United States and Japan in managing the world economy. Zbigniew Brzezinski, National Security Advisor to President Jimmy Carter, coined the expression 'Amerippon' to describe the close integration of the American and Japanese manufacturing, financial and commercial sectors and indeed the two economies as a whole. This image of the future has been enhanced by the steady rise in the yen's value compared to the US dollar, and the concomitant rise in Japanese GNP, now registering 20 per cent of world GNP.[14]

In Japan this image has been put forward most forcefully by former Prime Minister Yasuhiro Nakasone. In one of his meetings with President Reagan, he suggested that the two countries should forge a single community of the same destiny, although what he envisaged focused on security rather than on economic aspects of the bilateral relationship.[15] It must be noted that Japanese images of the future have tended to focus on Japan–US relations, to the dismay of Europeans and Asians, let alone other Third World countries. this tendency itself shows the strength of this second scenario.

Japan's roles in the 'bigemony' scenario may appear to some to be very similar to those envisaged in Pax Americana phase II. However, economic power becomes military power almost inevitably, and Japan does not constitute the historic exception to this rule.[16] But the form in which Japan's economic power will be translated into millitary power needs close attention. Under 'bigemony' the technical/economic/strategic cooperation-integration between the United States and Japan will become formidable, and of the largest scale in history. It is therefore not difficult to foresee, for instance, advanced fighter aircraft being developed jointly and manufactured primarily for Japanese use, with Japanese finance, though with American know-how, and also sold to third countries under the label, 'Made in the United States'. The large-scale strategic integration between these two countries as developed in the Pacific in the 1980s will come to be seen as a good testimony of the bigemonic roles Japan can play in security areas.

Japan's regional role in 'bigemony' is an acceleration of the features presented in Pax Americana phase II. A gigantic Pacific economic community will be forged, with Japan's role reminiscent of the role played by the corridor stretching from northern Italy through north-eastern France, the Rhineland and the Low Countries to southern Britain in modern European economic development. Under this scenario, the potentially heated contest between the United States and Japan over the structural framework of Pacific Asia's economic relationship with the United States will be largely dissipated. Currently, Pacific Asia faces increasingly clear alternatives as to its economic framework: either a US-led free-trade regime established through a bilateral agreement with the United States, or a regional community with *de facto* Japanese initiatives, which would try to retain a free-trade zone even if North America and Western Europe fell into the temptation of protectionism and regionalism of a malign kind.[17] Furthermore, the strategic integration of many countries in the region may make it hard to accommodate the Soviet Union within an invigorated bigemonic structure, thus relegating it to a far less imoprtant status than it currently occupies, unless some other countervailing moves are continuously taken. In this scenario Western Europe, though large in size and high in income level, will be increasingly localized within Europe and its immediate vicinity. This picture reminds one of Immanuel Wallerstein's scenario of the future predicting the formation of two *de facto* blocs, one comprising the United States, Japan and China, and the other both Western and Eastern Europe.[18]

3. Pax Consortis

Japan's third scenario protrays a world of many consortia in which the major actors proceed by busily forging coalitions to make policy adjustments and agreements among themselves – a world in which no single actor can dominate the rest. This scenario resembles Pax Americana II in its crude skeleton with its 'regimes' and 'cooperation under anarchy'. However, the major difference is that the thrust of the third scenario rests on the pluralistic nature of policy adjustment among the major actors, whereas that of the first conveys the desirability or necessity (or even the hoped-for inevitability) of 'administrative guid-ance' or 'moral leadership' by the state that is *primus inter pares* – the United States. This third image is favored by many Japanese, not least because Japan is averse to shouldering large security burdens. It is also favored because Japan is not completely happy about America ordering everyone around, especially when it only grudgingly admits its relative decline.

Kuniko Inoguchi, a Sophia University political scientist, artic-ulates this scenario most eloquently and forcefully in the con-text of the American debate on post-hegemonic stability of the international system. The image has also been put forward by former Vice-Minister Shinji Fukukawa of the Ministry of Inter-national Trade and Industry (MITI), which favours minimizing the role of military power.[19] Recently MITI and the Ministry of Foreign Affairs have been engaged in a degree of competition, with the Ministry of Foreign Affairs, conscious of the increasing intrusion by other ministries into foreign affairs, trying to use national security and the Western alliance as a stick to discipline other ministries which might otherwise move in an 'irresponsible' direction (as in the Toshiba machine case, when it came to light in 1987 that the Toshiba company had sold equipment to the Soviet Union which the United States claimed was in breach of the COCOM agreement on technology transfer). The image of Pax Consortis accords on the whole with the pacifist sentiments of most Japanese.

Japan's role in the Pax Consortis scenario is twofold. First, with the superpowers' strategic nuclear arsenals increasingly neutralized either by the *de facto* US–Soviet detente process or by technological breakthroughs, Japan's primary role is that of quiet economic diplomacy in forging coalitions and shaping policy adjustments among peers, no one of which is predominant. Secondly, Japan's role is that of helping to create a world free from military solutions. That would include, if possible, the diffusion of anti-nuclear defensive systems to all countries and the extension of massive economic aid tied to ceasefire or peace agreements between belligerent parties. Japan's primary regional role in this scenario would be that of coordinator or promoter of the interests of the Asian Pacific countries which have not been fully represented either in the UN system or in the economic institutions of the industrialized countries, such as the OECD. Japan's secondary regional role is that of moderator, especially in security areas.[20] This might include acting as an intermediary and attempting to achieve reconciliation between North and South Korea, or the provision of neutral peacekeeping forces in Cambodia and/or Afghanistan in order to facilitate reconstruction through massive aid flows from such multilateral institutions as the Asian Development Bank and the Gulf Cooperation Fund. Western Europe will loom larger in this scenario than in the other three. In line with its role in such forums as the Western seven-power summits, Western Europe will continue to play an even larger role, having been traditionally quite adept in those situations where multiple actors adjust conflicting interests. The increasing economic ties between Western Europe and Pacific Asia will also encourage thinking along the lines of this scenario.[21]

4. Pax Nipponica

A fourth image of the future, 'Pax Nipponica', was first put forward by Ezra Vogel, a Harvard sociologist, who in 1979 published a book entitled *Japan as Number One*. It is a world in which Japanese economic power reigns supreme. This scenario has been propagated by those Americans who are concerned about the visible contrast between the United States' relative loss of technological and manufacturing competitiveness and Japan's concomitant gain. Most recently, Ronald Morse of the US Library of Congress has published an article entitled 'Japan's drive to pre-eminence'.[22] This view has also been gaining power in Japan, reflecting both the noticeable rise in the value of the Japanese yen compared to the US dollar and other currencies and Japan's leading position as a creditor country. The steady rise of Japanese nationalism, in tandem with what the Japanese call the internationalization of Japan, is contributing to the strength of this scenario, because the intrusion of external economic and social forces into Japanese society stimulates nationalistic reactions against internationalization.

Japan's role in this scenario is best compared to that of Britain during the nineteenth century, when it played the role of balancer among the continental powers, its global commercial interests presumably helping it to fulfil this role. As for Pax Consortis in its fullest version, a prerequisite for the advent of Pax Nipponica is either the removal of the superpowers' strategic nuclear arsenals or the development of an anti-nuclear defense system. Without the neutralization of nuclear weapons, Japan's leading role in the security area would be minimized, and Pax Nipponica in its fullest form would not be realized. In this scenario, Japan's regional role will coincide with its global role, as its preeminent position will enable it to play the leading role in the Asian Pacific region as well.

These scenarios offer substantially different visions of Japan's future. I will now consider what conditions must prevail if they are to be realized.

Requirements for the four scenarios

To what extent are these scenarios feasible? Under what conditions will the scenarios come into being? In attempting to answer these questions, I will first identify three factors which seem to distinguish these scenarios from each other, and secondly, speculate on the feasibility of each scenario in the next 50 years.

There appear to be three major factors which are crucial in distinguishing these scenarios from each other – 1) the effective neutralization of strategic nuclear arsenals, 2) scientific and technological dynamism, and 3) the debt of history.

1. Neutralizing the nuclear arsenals

It is the arsenals of strategic nuclear forces that have allowed the United States and the Soviet Union to retain their superpower status and global influence. Whether these weapons will become obsolete – in other words, whether they cease to be a crucial factor determining global development – remains to be seen. Whether the United States or the Soviet Union or any other country will be able to arm itself with a defensive weapon system which makes it immune to nuclear attack is another question which needs to be answered, and the American SDI and its Soviet counterpart are directly related to this factor. The Conventional Defense Initiative (CDI) which the United States has recently proposed that Japan be jointly involved in may be included as a miniature version of a less ambitious yet more solid kind of effort. Ronald Reagan's fascination with the SDI and Japan's quiet effort to build the CDI may simply reflect what might be called a 'Maginot complex' surfacing again years after its failure.[23]

If such a revolutionary weapons system is realized, strategic nuclear arsenals will be neutralized. Unless this happens, the fourth scenario, Pax Nipponica, will have difficulty in emerging because while superpower status is based on ownership of strategic nuclear weapons, both the United States and the Soviet Union will remain superpowers despite all their economic difficulties. In a similar vein, the third scenario, Pax Consortis, will not materialize into a system comprising both economic and security regimes without a similar neutralization of strategic nuclear forces. With the disarmament process between the United States and the Soviet Union slowly making progress, strategic nuclear forces may not make much difference in determining global developments. There are those who, arguing in favor of Pax Consortis, maintain that nuclear weapons and even millitary power in general have already ceased to be a major factor in international politics and that economic interdependence has deepened sufficiently to make war an obsolete instrument for resolving conflicts of interests, at least among OECD countries and in direct East–West relations. Even granting that military power has become less important, I would argue that what is sometimes called the 'Europeanization of superpowers', in Christoph Bertram's phrase, will progress so slowly as to make it hard to envisage the fully fledged scenarios of Pax Consortis or Pax Nipponica inside the twentieth century. Needless to say, those who argue for Pax Consortis talk about it in a somewhat nebulous future most of the time.

2. Scientific and technological dynamism

Factor two concerns the innovative and inventive capacity of nations – how vigorous they are in making scientific and technological progress and in translating it to economic development. Needless to say, forecasting technological development is not easy. However, even a cursory examination of the social propensity to innovate seems to tell us that the Americans have been the most innovative nation, with the Japanese following on steadily behind. Such conditions as open competition, abundant opportunities, a strong spirit of individualism and freedom, and high social mobility, which are observed in the United States, compare very favorably to conditions in Japan.

There is another argument, however, which completely opposes this: that is to say, that Japanese technological innovation has been making steady progress. The following evidence is adduced for the argument:

1. The number of patents to utilize technological innovation exclusively for manufacturing obtained by Japanese companies and individuals in the United States has come very close to that of the United States itself. In 1987 the top three companies were all Japanese firms – Canon, Hitachi and Toshiba (in that order).[24]
2. More articles by Japan-based authors have appeared in *Chemical Abstracts* than by authors from any other country except the United States for several years.[25]
3. The United States in the first 30 years of this century produced as few as five Nobel prizewinners, which is about on a level with Japan's seven winners for the 40-year period since 1945.[26]

Yet as far as general innovativeness is concerned, the United

States seems likely to enjoy its dominant position at least until the end of the twentieth century. If this argument is sufficiently strong, then the first scenario gains force.

3. The legacy of history

Factor three is related to the memory of the peoples of the nations occupied in the Second World War of their treatment, primarily at the hands of the Germans and the Japanese. As the former Secretary-General of the Chinese Communist Party, Hu Yaobang, once said to Toyoko Yamakazi, a Japanese novelist, the memory of people who have suffered from war disappears only 80 years after the event. His evidence for this is the Boxer intervention in China in 1900, which has virtually been forgotten, whereas he argues that the memory of the second Sino-Japanese war of 1937–45 will not disappear from the memory of the Chinese for another 40 years.[27] With the question of their war-time atrocities still a politically controversial issue, as shown by international reaction to Japanese official visits to the Yasukuni shrine in Tokyo (which contained the remains of Japanese war criminals) and President Reagan's 1985 conciliatory visit to the Bitburg cemetery (which contained the graves of Waffen-SS men), Japan or West Germany cannot play a leading global role without facing many barriers.[28] Pax Nipponica is inherently difficult because of this factor.

The four scenarios reconsidered

Let me now examine the four scenarios in the light of these three factors.

Pax Americana II

Whether Pax Americana II is realized or not will critically depend on factor two – scientific/technical dynamism. The argument for this scenario tends to be based on the free spirit, open competition and dynamic character of American society, which it is thought will help the United States to reinvigorate its innovative and inventive capacity.

In my view this scenario has a fairly high feasibility if the present predicament is managed well. For that purpose two policies are essential: first, close Japan–US macroeconomic policy cooperation, and, secondly, the full-scale interlinking of the US economy with the Asian Pacific economies under US leadership. Whether the United States can achieve this without igniting Asian nationalism against it remains to be seen.[29]

'Bigemony'

The feasibility of 'bigemony' depends critically on factor three – the debt of history. In other words, whether Japanese pacifist feeling can be overcome and whether the East Asian neighbors can be at ease with Japanese leadership in regional and global security matters, even a leadership based on co-operation with the Americans, remains to be seen. To be feasible, therefore, this scenario requires very close friendship between the United States and Japan as a precondition for overcoming the debt of history problem. The argument against this scenario is that the steady progress of Japan–US economic integration and defense cooperation has been accompanied by recurrent and at times almost explosive friction between the two countries, which augurs ill for the future.

In my view, the 'bigemony' scenario can only progress slowly and steadily, in a moderate manner, as technological progress and economic dynamism push Japan and the United States closer together.

Pax Consortis

The feasibility of Pax Consortis depends cirtically on factor one – nuclear neutralization. This is conceivable in the distant future, but certainly not in the foreseeable future. For the two superpowers to relinquish superpower status and revert to less important roles will take time, even assuming that their decline has already begun. One may recall Edward Gibbon's remark that it took another 300 years for the Roman empire to disappear after its inevitable decline and demise were declared by Tacitus. It is utterly beyond speculation whether, and how, an unknown perfect anti-nuclear defensive weapon system might be developed and deployed. The weaker form of Pax Consortis, one could argue, is more feasible. One may cite the inability of the superpowers to have much influence on the course of events in Vietnam and Afghanistan, for example; the increasing importance of monetary and economic policy coordination and consultation among the major powers; increasing international collaboration in research and development; and the very frequent formation of consortia in manufacturing and financial acitivities. Needless to say, conventional forces will become more important when nuclear weapons are neutralized. Thus arms control – a kind of consortium – in conventional forces will become an important focus under Pax Consortis.

Pax Nipponica

The feasibility of Pax Nipponica depends critically on factors one and two – neutralization of nuclear weapons and scientific and technological dynamism. If both factors are realized together, the historical factor may become less important. But the difficulty of neutralizing nuclear weapons has already been mentioned. It must also be emphasized that the obstacles to Japan taking security leadership will not be easy to surmount. First, it will not be easy to persuade the overwhelmingly pacifist Japanese public. Secondly, it is not easy to see Japan shouldering the burden of the level of overseas armed forces the United States currently possesses for a prolonged period of time. It could easily lead Japan to suffer the kind of inefficiency that the Soviet Union has been so painfully experiencing. Thus estimates of Japan's likely scientific and technological dynamism will also affect the likelihood of Pax Nipponica.

In my view, Japan's innovative and inventive capacity for the next 10–20 years should not be underestimated. But beyond that period the expected fall in demographic dynamism and associated social malaises that are bound to arise, such as the overburdening of the small productive working population for extensive social welfare expenditure and for Japan's increased contributions for international public goods, seem to augur ill for this scenario.

To sum up. It seems to me that scenarios one and two – Pax Americana II and bigemony – are more likely than scenarios three and four in the intermediate term of 25 years, while in the longer term of 50 years a mixture of Pax Americana II and Pax Consortis seems more feasible. Of the two scenarios feasible in the medium term, Pax Americana II is the more desirable because it entails fewer risks to the United States as well as to the rest of the world. The effort necessary to sustain the US hegemonic position in its fullest form, whether alone or jointly with Japan or other allies, may cause more stresses than benefits. In the larger term, a soft landing on a Pax Consortis seems desirable.

Conclusion

These four scenarios are, admittedly, incomplete. Yet their delineation is useful in order to know better what kind of futures the Japanese have in mind in their assiduous yet uncertain search for their place in the world. Some readers may be struck by the fact that these scenarios reflect peculiarly Japanese aspirations and apprehensions. The weight of the past not only lingers on, but fundamentally constrains the Japanese conception of the world. Any drastic restructuring of Japan's foreign relations away from the ties with the United States seems virtually impossible to the majority of Japanese. It is instructive to learn that in Japan only 7.2 per cent of the population are neutralists, who want to abrogate the country's security treaty with the United States, while in West Germany as many as 44 per cent are neutralists.[30]

The same thing can be said of the three major factors. First, the debt of history to the Pacific Asian neighbors has been deeply felt as a major constraining factor in our scenarios. It is as if an anti-Japanese alliance in Pacific Asia were always ready to be forged, despite the near half-century since the war, just because Japan once crossed a certain threshold of misconduct. Secondly, the neutralization of nuclear weapons has been the dream of most Japanese since 1945, when two nuclear bombs were dropped on two Japanese cities. Thirdly, the innovative and inventive capacity of nations is one of those things many Japanese have long felt lacking within themselves. Perhaps reflecting that, they waver between unnaturally timid and exceedingly bold estimates of their own scientific and technological capacity.

Some may argue that my overall scenario – a soft-landing scenario proceeding from Pax Americana II to the Pax Consortis – is more than mildly optimistic. This may be true. It is arguable that this optimism is somewhat unfounded when the United States, the architect of the post-war order, is beset by severe problems. The point is that a large majority of responsible Japanese leaders have found it virtually impossible to think beyond a world where the United States is of primary importance to Japan and where the Japan–US friendship is a major pillar of global stabiliity. My delineation of four scenarios, including the Pax Nipponica and bigemony, should not be understood as a disclosure of non-existent plans for Japan to become a world supremo, or co-supremo. Rather, it should be interpreted as a manifestation of the kind of independent impulse long suppressed, yet only recently allowed to appear on a very small scale in tandem with Japan's rise as a global economic power. The Japanese are perplexed as they continue to rise in influence. Under what combination of the four scenarios Japan will stand up on the world stage remains a matter for our common and compelling interest.

Notes

1. Inoguchi Takashi, *Tadanori to ikkoku hanei shugi o koete* (Beyond free ride and prosperity-in-one-country-ism) (Tokyo: Toyo keizai shimosha, 1987); Inoguchi Takashi, 'Tenkanki Nihon no kadai' (Japan's tasks at a time of transition), *Nihon keizai shimbun*, 1, 8, 15, 22 and 29 November 1987.
2. Takashi Inoguchi, 'The ideas and structures of foreign policy: looking ahead with caution', in Takashi Inoguchi and Daniel I. Okimoto (eds.), *The Political Economy of Japan, Volume 2: The Changing International Context* (Stanford: Stanford University Press, 1988), pp. 23–63, 490–500; Takashi Inoguchi, 'Japan's images and options: not a challenger, but a supporter', *Journal of Japanese*

Studies, Winter 1986, Vol. 12, No. 1, pp. 95–119, included as Chapter 1 of this volume; Takashi Inoguchi, 'Japan's foreign policy background', in Herbert J. Ellison (ed.) *Japan and the Pacific Quadrille* (Boulder, Colo.: Westview, 1987), pp. 81–105.

3. Murray Sayle, 'The powers that might be: Japan is no sure bet as the next global top dog', *Far Eastern Economic Review*, 4 August 1988, pp. 38–43.

4. Department of Public Relations, Office of the Prime Minister, *Gaiko ni kansuru yoron chosa* (Opinion poll on diplomacy) (Tokyo: Office of the Prime Minister, April 1988).

5. Watanuki Joji *et al.*, *Nihonjin no senkyo kodo* (Japanese electoral behaviour) (Tokyo: University of Tokyo Press, 1986).

6. Takashi Inoguchi, 'Trade, technology and security: implications for east Asia and the West', *Adelphi Papers* (London: International Institute for Strategic Studies), Spring 1987, No. 218, pp. 39–55, Chapter 4 of this volume; Takashi Inoguchi, 'The legacy of a weathercock prime minister', *Japan Quarterly*, Oct.–Dec. 1987, Vol. 34, No. 4, pp. 363–70, Chapter 3 of this volume.

7. When the 1987 fiscal budget draft was revealed early in 1987, it surpassed the 1 per cent limit. But because in 1987 GNP increased much more vigorously, defense expenditure became less than 1 per cent of GNP at the end of the 1987 fiscal year. On the opinion polls, see Nisihira Sigeki, *Yoron ni miru dosedaishi* (Contemporary history through opinion polls) (Tokyo: Brain shuppan, 1987), p. 295.

8. *Asahi shimbun*, 30 October 1987; see also Chuma Kiyofuku, 'Nihon no yukue o kangaeru' (Thinking about Japan's future direction), *Sekai,* December 1987 pp. 85–98.

9. Inoguchi Takashi, 'Tenkanki Nihon no kadai', *Nihon keizai shimbun*, 15 November 1987.

10. Stephen Krasner (ed.), *International Regimes* (Ithaca, NY: Cornell University Press, 1983); Robert O. Keohane, *After Hegemony: Cooperation and Discord in the World Political Economy* (Princeton, NJ: Princeton University Press, 1984); Kenneth A. Oye (ed.), *Cooperation Under Anarchy* (Princeton, NJ: Princeton University Press, 1985).

11. Bruce M. Russett, 'The mysterious case of vanishing hegemony: or, is Mark Twain really dead?', *International Organization,* Spring 1985, Vol. 39, No. 2, pp. 207–31; Susan Strange, 'The persistent myth of lost hegemony', *International Organization*, Autumn 1987, Vol. 41, No. 4, pp. 551–74; Paul Kennedy, *The Rise and Fall of the Great Powers* (New York: Random House, 1987); Joseph S. Nye, Jr, *Bound to Lead: The Changing Nature of American Power,* (New York: Basic Books, 1990); Henry Nau, *The Myth of America's Decline: Leading the World Economy into the 1990s* (New York: Oxford University Press, 1990); Richard Rosecrance, *America's Economic Resurgence: A Bold New Strategy* (New York: Harper and Row, 1990); Charles

Doron, *System in Crisis* (New York: Cambridge University Press, 1991).

12. Amaya Naohiro, *Nihon wa dokoe ikunoka* (Whither Japan?) (Tokyo: PHP Institute, 1987); Murakami Yasusuke, 'After hegemony', *Chuo koron*, November 1985.

13. Colin I. Bradford and William Branson (eds.), *Trade and Structural Change in Pacific Asia* (Chicago Ill.: University of Chicago Press, 1987): Peter Drysdale, *International Economic Pluralism: Economic Policy in East Asia and the Pacific* (Sydney: George Allen & Unwin, 1988).

14. Robert Gilpin, *War and Change in World Politics* (Cambridge: Cambridge University Press, 1981); Robert Gilpin, *The Political Economy of International Relations* (Princeton, NJ: Princeton University Press, 1987).

15. Inoguchi, 'The legacy of a weathercock prime minister', *op. cit.*

16. Kennedy, *The Rise and Fall of the Great Powers, op. cit.*

17. Takashi Inoguchi, 'Shaping and sharing Pacific dynamism', Chapter 6 of this Volume.

18. Immanuel Wallerstein, 'Friends as foes', *Foreign Policy,* Fall 1980, pp. 119–31.

19. Inoguchi Kuniko, *Posuto haken sisutemu to Nihon no sentaku* (An emerging post-hegemonic system: choices for Japan) (Tokyo: Chikuma shobo, 1987); Fukukawa Shinji, *21 Seiki no Nihon no sentaku* (Japan's choice in the twenty-first century) (Tokyo: TBS Britannica, 1990).

20. Inoguchi, *Tadanori to ikkoku hanei shugi o koete, op. cit.*

21. Inoguchi, 'Shaping and sharing Pacific dynamism', *op. cit.*

22. Ezra Vogel, *Japan as Number One* (Cambridge, Mass.: Harvard University Press, 1979); Ezra Vogel, 'Pax Nipponica?', *Foreign Affairs*, Spring 1986, Vol. 64, No. 4, pp. 752–67; Ronald A. Morse, 'Japan's drive to pre-eminence', *Foreign Policy*, Winter 1987–8, No. 69, pp. 3–21.

23. On the CDI pushed by the US Congress see David C. Morrison, 'Earth wars', *National Journal,* 1 August 1987, pp. 1,972–5; Ronald L. Kerber and Donald N. Frederiksen, 'The Conventional Defense Initiative/balanced technology initiative', *Defense Issues*, 1987, Vol. 2, No. 36, pp. 1–5. I am grateful to Jefferson Seabright for enabling me to read these and other related materials.

24. *Nihon keizai shimbun*, 26 March 1988.

25. Negishi Masamitsu, 'Gakujutsu Kenkyu ronbum su no Kokusai hikaku chosa' (International comparison of academic articles), Gakuiutsu Geppo (Monthly Bulletin of Academic Affairs) Vol. 41, No. 7 (July 1988), pp. 588–95). *Asahi shimbun*, evening edition, 24 March 1988.

26. Peter Katzenstein, 'Supporter states in the international system: Japan and West Germany', paper prepared for presentation for the conference, 'Globalized business activities and the international economy'.

27. Yamazaki Toyoko, 'Shimidarake no shidosha' (The leader full of stains), *Bungei Shunju*, May 1985, pp. 23–6.
28. Research Institute of International Trade and Industry, Tokyo, 23–4 June 1988; Hanns Maull, 'Germany and Japan', *Foreign Affairs*, Vol. 69, No. 5 (Winter 1990/91, pp. 91–106).
29. In view of this, whether or not Japan joins the East Asian Economic Grouping, a scheme proposed by Malaysia and the ASEAN countries in order to enhance their bargaining position *vis-à-vis* the United States, pressure toward further market liberalization must be watched.
30. On the West German figure, see 'Disarmament is a long word and takes a long time to say', *The Economist*, 30 July 1988, pp. 39–41. On the Japanese figure see Sayle, 'The powers that might be', *op. cit.*

Select Bibliography

1. The study of international relations presumes some knowledge of history. The more familiar one is with history, the better. This applies especially to the study of Japan's international relations. However, due to limitations of space, I suggest only the following general books.

William G. Beasley, *The Rise of Modern Japan* (London: Weidenfeld and Nicolson, 1990).

William Horsley and Roger Buckley, *Nippon: The New Superpower: Japan since 1945* (London: BBC Books, 1990).

Edwin O. Reischauer, *The Japanese Today: Change and Continuity* (Cambridge, Mass.: The Belknap Press, 1988).

The Cambridge History of Japan, Volumes 5 and 6 (Cambridge: Cambridge University Press, 1989 and 1988, respectively), provides the best authoritative account in English of the two most recent centuries for those wishing to know more.

2. The study of international relations requires good understanding of domestic workings of the economy, society, and politics. This point is especially important to any analysis of Japan's international relations. Although I surmise that many readers of this book may not now be tempted to read these works, I believe they will appreciate the listing below when they do choose to read further.

Masahiko Aoki, *Information, Incentives, and Bargaining in the Japanese Economy* (Cambridge: Cambridge University Press, 1988).

Bela Balassa and Marcus Noland, *Japan in the World Economy* (Washington: Institute for International Economics, 1988).

Theodore C. Bestor, *Neighborhood Tokyo* (Stanford: Stanford University Press, 1989).

Kent Calder, *Crisis and Compensation: Public Policy and Political Stability in Japan, 1949–1986* (Princeton: Princeton University Press, 1988).

Gerald Curtis, *The Japanese Way of Politics* (New York: Columbia University Press, 1988).

Ronald Dore, *Flexible Rigidities: Industrial Policy and Structural Adjustment in the Japanese Economy, 1970–80* (Stanford: Stanford University Press, 1986).

Chalmers Johnson, *MITI and the Japanese Miracle: The Growth of Industrial Policy, 1925–1975* (Stanford: Stanford University Press, 1982).

Edward J. Lincoln, *Japan: Facing Economic Maturity* (Washington: Brookings Institution, 1988).

Edward J. Lincoln, *Japan's Unequal Trade* (Washington: Brookings Institution, 1990).

Gavan McCormack and Yoshio Sugimoto (eds), *Modernization and Beyond: The Japanese Trajectory* (Cambridge: Cambridge University Press, 1988).

William R. Nester, *The Foundation of Japanese Power: Continuities, Changes, Challenges* (London: Macmillan, 1990).

Daniel I. Okimoto, *Between MITI and the Market: Japanese Industrial Policy for High Technology Industries* (Stanford: Stanford University Press, 1989).

Hugh Patrick (ed.), *Japan's High Technology Industries: Lessons and Limitations of Industrial Policy* (Seattle: University of Washington Press, 1986).

T.J. Pempel (ed.), *Uncommon Democracies: The One-Party Dominant Regimes* (Ithaca: Cornell University Press, 1990).

Susan Pharr, *Losing Face: Status Politics in Japan* (Berkeley: University of California Press, 1990).

Kenneth B. Pyle (ed.), *The Trade Crisis: How Will Japan Respond?* (Seattle: Society for Japanese Studies, 1986).

Steven Reed, *Japanese Prefectures and Policymaking* (Pittsburgh: University of Pittsburgh Press, 1986).

Frances McCall Rosenbluth, *Financial Politics in Contemporary Japan* (Ithaca: Cornell University Press, 1987).

Richard Samuels, *The Business of the Japanese State: Energy Markets in Comparative and Historical Perspective* (Ithaca: Cornell University Press, 1987).

Michele Schmiegelow and Henrik Schmiegelow, *Strategic Pragmatism: Japanese Lessons in the Use of Economic Theory* (New York: Praeger, 1989).

Rob Steven, *Classes in Contemporary Japan* (Cambridge: Cambridge University Press, 1983).

J.A.A. Stockwin, *Japan: Divided Politics in a Growth Economy* (New York: Norton, 1975).

Shinya Sugiyama, *Japan's Industrialization in the World Economy, 1859-99* (London: Athlone, 1988).

Ezra Vogel, *Japan as Number One: Lessons for America* (Cambridge: Harvard University Press, 1979).

Kozo Yamamura (ed.), *Japan's Economic Structure: Should It Change?* (Seattle: Society for Japanese Studies, 1990).

Kozo Yamamura and Yasukichi Yasuba (eds.), *The Political Economy of Japan, Volume 1: The Domestic Transformation* (Stanford: Stanford University Press, 1987).

Karel van Wolferen, *The Enigma of Japanese Power* (London: Macmillan, 1989).

3. Until recently, Japan's international relations have not been the subject of intense curiosity outside Japan. Hence the relative paucity of books in English to meet the current strong demand.

Michael Blaker, *Japanese International Negotiating Style* (New York: Columbia University Press, 1977).

Robert W. Barnett, *Beyond War: Japan's Concept of Comprehensive National Security* (Washington: Pergamon-Brassey's, 1984).

J.W.M. Chapman, R. Drifte, and I.T.M. Gow, *Japan's Quest for Comprehensive Security: Defense, Diplomacy, Dependence* (New York: St. Martin's Press, 1983).

Reinhard Drifte, *Japan's Foreign Policy* (London: Routledge, 1990).

Ellen L. Frost, *For Richer, For Poorer: The New U.S.-Japan Relationship* (New York: Council on Foreign Relations, 1987).

Takashi Inoguchi and Daniel Okimoto (eds), *The Political Economy of Japan, Volume 2: The Changing International Context* (Stanford: Stanford University Press, 1988).

Akira Iriye and Warren I. Cohen (eds), *The United States and Japan in the Postwar World* (Lexington: University of Kentucky Press, 1989).

Kenjiro Ishikawa, *Japan and the Challenge of Europe 1992* (London: Royal Institute of International Affairs, 1990).

Shafiqul Islam, *Yen for Development* (New York: Council on Foreign Relations, 1991).

Ramons H. Myers and Mark R. Peattie (eds), *The Japanese Colonial Empire, 1895–1945* (Princeton: Princeton University Press, 1984).

William Nester, *Japan's Growing Power over East Asia and the World Economy: Ends and Means* (London: Macmillan, 1990).

Kathleen Newland (ed.), *The International Relations of Japan* (London: Macmillan, 1990).

Ian Nish, *Japanese Foreign Policy, 1869–1942* (London: Routledge and Kegan Paul, 1977).

Kazushi Ohkawa and Gustav Ranis (eds), *Japan and the Developing Countries* (New York: Basil Blackwell, 1985).

Hisahiko Okazaki, *A Grand Strategy for Japanese Defense* (Lanham, Maryland: University Press of America, 1986).

Robert M. Orr, Jr, *The Emergence of Japan's Foreign Aid Power* (New York: Columbia University Press, 1990).

Myles L. Robertson, *Soviet Policy Towards Japan* (Cambridge: Cambridge University Press, 1988).

Shiro Saito, *Japan at the Summit. Japan's Role in the Western Alliance and Asian Pacific Cooperation* (London: Routledge, 1990).

Robert A. Scalapino (ed.), *The Foreign Policy of Modern Japan* (Berkeley: University of California Press, 1977).

Masahide Shibusawa, *Japan and the Asian Pacific Region* (London: Croom Helm, 1984).

John Welfield, *An Empire in Decline: Japan in the Postwar American Alliance System* (London: Athlone Press, 1988).

Allen S. Whiting, *China Eyes Japan* (Berkeley: University of California Press, 1989).

4. A number of periodicals that often deal with Japan's international relations are worth mentioning.

Japan Forum
Journal of the Japanese and International Economies
Journal of Japanese Studies
Monumenta Nipponica

Asian Survey
Pacific Affairs

Pacific Review
Journal of Asian Studies
Journal of Northeast Asian Studies

Foreign Affairs
Foreign Policy
International Affairs
International Organization
International Studies Quarterly
Review of International Studies
World Politics

Japan Echo
Look Japan
Economic Eye
Journal of Japanese Trade and Industry
Japanese Review of International Affairs

Index